The Book of Ke

BIRD'S-EYE VIEW OF THE KINGDOM OF KERRY

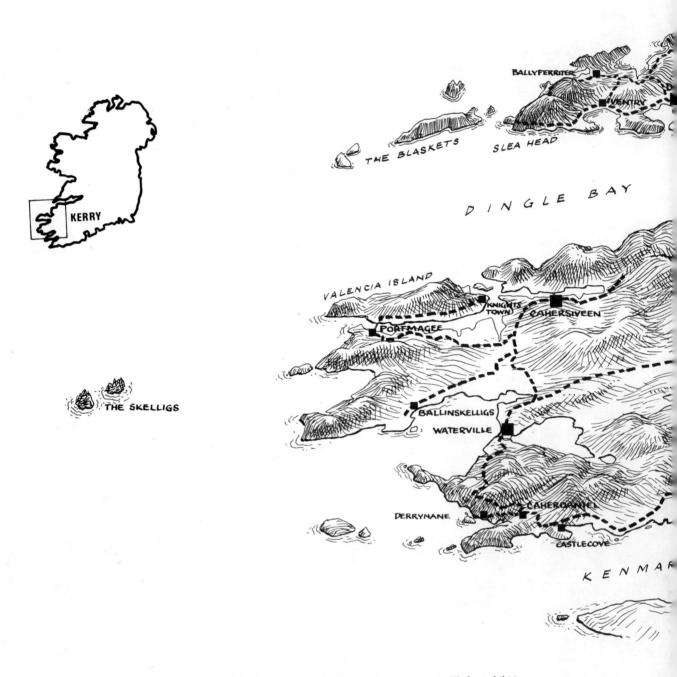

Previous page: A warrior defends the ancient kingdom at the entrance to a Tralee exhibition.

To Geraldine
Who helped to navigate the boreens.

MAIN FESTIVALS IN COUNTY KERRY		
APRIL	Kenmare Walking Festival	Easter
	Easter Folk Festival, Killarney	
MAY	Killarney Spring Horse Racing	mid-May
	Listowel Writers' Week	end of May
JUNE	Tarbert Island Regatta	end of June
	Ballybunion Bachelor Festival	end of June
JULY	Killarney Horse Racing	mid-July
	Brandon Regatta	mid-July
AUGUST	Dingle Races	early August
	Puck Fair, Killorglin	mid-August
	Dingle Regatta	late August
	Rose of Tralee Festival	late August
	Tralee Races	late August
SEPTEMBER	Listowel Racing Festival	end of September
	Listowel Harvest Festival	end of September
OCTOBER	Daniel O'Connell Assoc. Workshop	end of October

Above: Entering County Kerry at Tarbert, and facing page: the town of Sneem

The Book of Kerry

TOWNS AND VILLAGES IN THE KINGDOM

Arthur Flynn

DESIGN AND ILLUSTRATION: JAN DE FOUW

WOLFHOUND PRESS

First published 1993 by
WOLFHOUND PRESS
68 Mountjoy Square, Dublin 1

British Library Cataloguing in Publication Data
Flynn, Arthur
    Book of Kerry: Towns and Villages of the Kingdom
    I. Title
    914.19604
    ISBN 0-86327-372-6

Book and cover design: Jan de Fouw
Typesetting: Wolfhound Press. Printed in the Republic of Ireland by Colour Books, Dublin.

Illustration: Bird's-eye view map, photographs and line drawings by Jan de Fouw. Maps pages 15, 43, 63 and 91 by Jeannette Dunne. Photographs on pages 17, 27, 51, 57, 59, 61, 65, 67 (right), 69 (bottom), 77, 78, 79, 81, 89, 101 (right) courtesy of the author. Photographs on pages 14, 18, 29, 30, 32, 35, 47, 57 (bottom), 87 (top and right), 90, and top and bottom front cover photographs by kind permission of Bord Fáilte. Centre cover photograph courtesy of MacMonagles, Killarney Printing Works Ltd, Killarney. Otherwise as credited.

Acknowledgements: *I would like to thank the following for their assistance in my preparation of this book:* Stephen Cotter, The Plough, Milltown; Dan Keane; Bryan MacMahon; Christine Fitzgerald; John B. Keane; Fr John O'Connell; Fiona Poole; Fr J.A. Gaughan; Tim Brady; Dr Michael Fanning, Dingle; Marie Allman, Causeway; Norah O'Sullivan, Dingle, Dymphna Morgan, Trassa and Kieran Kelliher, Castlemaine; Garrett Flynn for reading and advising on text; Fr Kieran O'Shea; Áine O'Sullivan; John O'Mahony, Jim Smulders, Ardfert; Maura Corcoran, Oireachtas Library, Kerry Airport Plc; Kerry Co-op; Office of Public Works; Cork/Kerry Tourism; Bord Fáilte; Thomas O'Connor, Local History Department, Tralee Library; Michael Kelleher and Eileen Murray, Bray Library; The National Library, Dublin; Kathleen Browne, Kerry County Librarian and the staff of Dingle, Listowel and Killarney Libraries. Particular thanks to Florence Armstrong, Geraldine Flynn, Damian Flynn and Noel Rowsome for proofreading. I am also grateful to Seamus Cashman and Josephine O'Donovan of Wolfhound Press for their patience and guidance.

Cross and ogham stone at Kilmalkedar, Dingle

Caherconree, near Camp,
Dingle peninsula

Preface

Despite the encroachment of commercialism and advancing technology, Kerry maintains much of its primitive beauty and is indisputably the tourism capital of Ireland.

County Kerry extends from Tarbert on the Shannon, to Kerry Head, its western boundary, to the estuary of the Kenmare River. There are no definitive landmarks to its eastern and southern boundaries. The name Kerry derives from the descendants of Ciar (the son of Fergus and Queen Maeve of Connaught), who were called Ciarraidhe, and their territory of Ciarraighe. Other sources indicate that it originated from the word Cairich, meaning rocky, and the fact that the county is covered with valleys and mountains, including the highest mountain in Ireland, Carrantuohill, standing at 3,414 feet, would give credence to that theory. Famous Kerrymen include Cú Raoi Mac Daire who was King of West Munster (which is now called Kerry) when Conor Mac Nessa was King of Ulster. The county has long been associated with St Brendan, as he was born, lived and died there. He was an avid sailor and founded a monastery at Ardfert. Tradition has it that he reached America several centuries before Christopher Columbus.

The county is rich in ancient sites and relics of prehistoric, pagan and Christian origin. There are many raths, believed by some to have been the abode of fairies, for whom the Irish name is Sidhe (pronounced Shee) or 'people of the hills'. Staigue Fort at Castlecove is the best example of these historic stone fortresses. Throughout the county there are also many gallauns, stone circles, souterrains and cromlechs. Close to Kenmare lies a large cromlech and there is another fine example at Killarney. A vast number of ogham stones have been discovered in the county, principally at Aghadoe and Parknasilla. Ogham characters are an early form of writing — perhaps pre-Christian — and are formed by straight lines cut in the stone at right and obtuse angles to a longer central and upright line, generally formed by the angle of the stone.

The largest and most prosperous towns are Tralee, Killarney, Listowel and Dingle. From earliest days the county was known abroad, as Ptolemy wrote of Kenmare iron in the second century. A group of Anglo-Norman adventurers conquered most of North Kerry in the thirteenth century, displacing natives and granting their land to their own knights. The southern portion was formerly owned by the O'Sullivans, O'Mahonys and O'Donoghues. The Earl of Desmond was appointed Keeper of the Peace by the Crown in 1388 but Gerald, the sixteenth Earl, rebelled against Elizabeth and this part of the county was not finally subdued until 1691. With the influx of foreign traders there was a mixture of Spanish and Portuguese blood in people living close to the coast. Kerry became a county in 1606.

In September 1588 ships of the Spanish Armada fought a series of running battles with the British fleet. Heading north around Scotland and down the west coast of Ireland en route back to Spain they were battered by storms and sought refuge in sheltered inlets. Many of these vessels were wrecked off the coast from Donegal to Kerry. At least two of their ships were sunk in the Blasket Sound and two others off Valentia Island with a loss of nine hundred lives.

In a report to the Lord Lieutenant on the state of Kerry, made early in the seventeenth century, by Lord Herbert and two other Justices of the Peace for the county, the justices complained of the conditions of the roads in the three baronies of Iveragh, Dunkerron and Glanarough. Many landlords did much to improve and develop areas of the county: Sir William Petty opened an iron works and fishery in Kenmare, Lord Kenmare brought linen and woollen industries to Killarney and Walter Hussey was extremely energetic in Dingle. One of the best known absentee landlords was the Earl of Shelbourne, who became Prime Minister of England in 1782. He considered that the best remedy for Irish poverty and discontent was the development of agriculture. Under his direction medals were designed and awarded which served as an example to the peasants. On one side was a humble cabin with barefooted children coming out the door while on the reverse was a prosperous-looking farm.

Arthur Young wrote in 1779: 'The state of the poor in the whole county of Kerry represented as exceedingly miserable, and owing to the conduct of men of property, who are apt to lay the blame on what they call land pirates, or men who offer the highest rate.' Young also observed that the clothing of the peasants was in the main black or navy blue and that beggars gathered at popular resorts like Killarney or the Puck Fair in Killorglin.

Several areas of the county were to develop as tourist centres, particularly Killarney, Dingle and Ballybunion. *Hall's Ireland* reported that 'the tourist in Kerry will be most agreeably disappointed if he imagines that his source of information and pleasure in visiting it are limited to the far-famed lakes. Kerry abounds in natural wonders, and the beauty and grandeur of the scenes to which we have more specially referred may certainly be equalled, if not surpassed in other, although less celebrated, districts of the country.'

In the mid 1800s, due to famine and lack of employment, workhouses were opened throughout the county in Listowel, Kenmare, Killarney, Tralee and Cahirciveen. Due to the high cost of maintaining paupers in workhouses it was agreed that they would be given free passage to America. Between 1830 and 1861, some 63,100 people emigrated from Co Kerry. Most were uneducated and from the labouring classes.

The introduction of the railway, with a series of branch lines throughout the county from the 1850s, made remote areas more accessible. However, following the Transport Act of 1958 CIE had to prune its operation and close many lines, including those to Kenmare, Valentia Island, Dingle and Fenit.

Atrocities dot the history of County Kerry. In 1580 an incident occurred which became known as the 'Massacre of Smerwick Harbour', in which a strong English force under Lord Grey coldbloodedly killed six hundred Italian, Basque, Spanish and Irish prisoners. (At the end of the sixteenth century, troops from many European countries supported the Irish against British forces.) A bitter campaign was fought during the Civil War of 1922-23. In one incident in Knocknagoshel five men were tied to a landmine and blown up. This act of treachery was followed by savage reprisals throughout the county.

Over the years many aspects of life in Kerry have been captured on film, from Sidney Olcott's pioneering efforts in 1911 to Tom Cooper's production of *The Dawn* with the assistance of local amateurs in Killarney. The best remembered film is David Lean's epic drama *Ryan's Daughter* which magnificently captured the rugged landscapes and has since proved an enormous tourist draw for the entire Dingle peninsula. Recently another major film, *Far and Away*, was filmed in the same location.

Many prominent personalities have had connections with the county, the most important being Daniel O'Connell. He was born at Cahirciveen and the family lived in a fine house at Caherdaniel. From here he defended the poor in court and organised rallies to achieve Catholic emancipation; he was the first Irish Catholic to take a seat in the British Parliament. Roger Casement will always be associated with Kerry as his ill-fated landing from a German submarine took place on Banna Beach on Good Friday 1916. Casement was brought to London for trial, found guilty as a traitor and hanged. Literary figures have also been prominent, particularly in North Kerry. Listowel has produced such distinguished figures as the Abbey playwright George Fitzmaurice, novelist Maurice Walsh, as well as contemporaries like novelist Bryan MacMahon, playwright John B. Keane, and in nearby Ballylongford the poet Brendan Kennelly.

~

For the past twenty years, Kerry has been a second home to me. Its attractions for me are many, from the sheer unspoilt beauty and uncluttered roads to unpolluted beaches, rivers and lakes. The greatest appeal for me has been the warmth and friendliness of its people and its colourful characters, full of humour and tall stories.

From over those years many personal memories spring to mind. Having my car marooned for three days as Killorglin throbbed with Puck Fair. A Kerry wake when everyone was invited into the house to enjoy the chat, music, Guinness and ham sandwiches. Enjoying the crack and music in John B. Keane's pub. Listening to the late Sean McCarthy regaling a hushed room with his amazing travels and exploits. Walking through the streets of Listowel with Bryan MacMahon, as he rattled off the history and roots of every family and building. A cultural coach tour through the boreens of North Kerry. Musical evenings around a turf fire as elderly Gaelic speakers passed musical instruments between them. The kitchen, where furniture was pushed back to make space for impromptu set dances. The pageantry and festive atmosphere of the Rose of Tralee. The indescribable beauty of a sunset over the Lakes of Killarney. Listening to graphic descriptions of Kerry's glorious days of winning the All-Ireland. A leisurely stroll along the wind-swept beach at Inch. Walking up Brandon pier with an armful of fresh mackerel. Cooking trout over an open fire on Ventry strand. Breathlessly trying to keep up with my children as they sprinted up to the summit of a snow-capped Mount Brandon. The first sighting of Fungie the dolphin. A spine-tingling journey by curragh to the Blaskets.

Kerry is rich in folklore and heritage. I hope that this book transmits some of that wealth, and that my personal choices of places worth visiting help you savour the warmth of Kerry's welcome.

Kerry's Story

At the end of the ice age, Mesolithic man came to Ireland, and traces of Mesolithic culture have been found near Inch strand and Castlegregory, and at Ballyeagh near Ballybunion. The Neolithic, or later stone age, culture began in Ireland around 6,500 years ago, leaving passage graves such as Newgrange in the Boyne Valley. Two thousand years later, bronze age man was to leave mine workings, traces of houses and fields, assembly places, copper and bronze tools and weapons, rock carvings and great wedge tombs scattered across Kerry. Dating from about 500 BC, old roads, field systems, stone and promontory forts and ring, or earthen, forts can be seen, and there remains an extraordinary body of Irish legends from this period that became the basis of much of early Irish literature for the next 2,000 years.

Christianity came to Kerry in the fifth century AD, and many of the sites date from the following centuries — monasteries, inscribed crosses, tombstones, and island sites such as the spectacular Skellig Michael. From around 800, Christian monasteries became a focal point for those seeking refuge from Viking invaders, and the round towers built at this time can still be seen, including one at Rattoo.

In the struggles of the eleventh and twelfth centuries to establish a single native kingdom of Ireland, three of the Gaelic ruling families established themselves in Kerry: MacCarthy, southwards from Killarney, O'Donoghue around Killarney and O'Sullivan around the Kenmare river.

In 1170, the Normans came to Ireland under Strongbow — the beginning of an English military presence. They quickly overran most of the island, and assimilated with the native Gaels. By the thirteenth century, the anglo-Normans conquered the north and west of Kerry, but for nearly four hundred years failed to penetrate further. The Anglo-Norman Fitzgeralds, who became Earls of Desmond, established strongholds in the Castleisland and Tralee areas, bringing in tenants from abroad, known as Planters, to occupy their territory — hence such names as Brown, Ashe, Ferriter. Until the sixteenth century, they maintained a feudal independence.

Below: Memorial to Ireland's dead at Ballyseedy near Tralee Facing page: Fishing on the River Maine

By the time Henry VIII came to the throne, Ireland was ruled by chieftains who owed nominal allegiance to England. His daughter, Queen Elizabeth I, was to enforce that allegiance in wars that raged across the country and culminated in Kerry. The general post-Elizabethan settlement joined the north and south parts to form the county of Kerry in 1606. In 1649, Oliver Cromwell led a powerful force to subdue Ireland. The period of fighting which followed, known as the Cromwellian era, ended the political and economic power of the great Gaelic families and established a Protestant ascendancy.

At the end of the seventeenth century, a series of harsh laws known as the Penal Laws were in force against Catholics (who formed the majority of the population) prohibiting them from holding any office of state, voting, buying or holding a long lease on land, etc. By the late eighteenth century, barely 5% of land remained in Catholic hands. It was not until 1829 that Daniel O'Connell from Derrynane, Co Kerry, won Catholic Emancipation for Ireland, with the repeal of these laws.

In the 1840s, the potato crop failed all over Ireland, resulting in the Great Irish Famine. The combination of disease, starvation and the heavy emigration that followed reduced Kerry's population by almost two-thirds, with the Iveragh and Beara peninsulas losing three-quarters of their population.

In modern times, Kerry mirrors the history of Ireland very fully, from the Fenian rebellions of the nineteenth century (led by the Irish Republican Brotherhood — IRB — and the Irish Republican Army — IRA, not to be confused with the modern-day terrorist IRA who bear the same name), to the 1916 Rising centred on Dublin's General Post Office, the arrival of the infamous Black and Tan military force from Britain, through the War of Independence (1919-21) ending with the Anglo-Irish Treaty of 1921 that established a 26-county republic, and the bitterly divisive Civil War (1922-23) between Pro- and Anti-Treaty forces which left its mark on Irish and Kerry politics for the next half-century.

In the latter half of the twentieth century, Kerry reflects all that is best in a changing modern Ireland — a fine linkage of traditional culture and sporting life, thriving and coexisting in a modern context with booming tourist and food industries, and successful local businesses reaching international markets. [— J. O'D]

Left: On Skellig Michael
Below: Ancient kist grave near Waterville

The Ring of Kerry

One of the most popular drives for tourists in the entire country is the coast road which runs around the shore of the Iveragh Peninsula, the central and largest of County Kerry's peninsulas. It is known as the Ring of Kerry. Completing the entire circle from Killarney on the main road is approximately 110 miles, but any traveller would be advised to make some worthwhile detours en route. The journey can be undertaken clockwise through Kenmare or anti-clockwise out the Killorglin Road. My own favourite direction is anti-clockwise and I will follow that route, noting the most interesting diversions. It is important to pick a clear, dry day to experience the scenery at its best. On an inclement day entire mountains and valleys can be blotted out by mist.

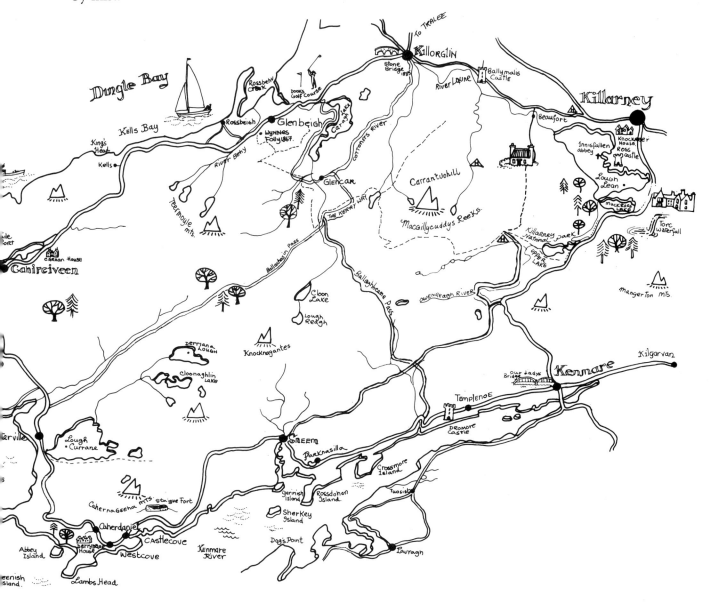

... THE ONE LONE PUCK (GOAT) HEADED FOR KILLORGLIN ...

Killorglin

Killorglin, a hilly town overlooking the River Laune, is the gateway to the Iveragh peninsula. To the south are the dominant Macgillycuddy Reeks range of mountains. On the eastern side of the river, Dromavela Church was erected and dedicated to St Lawrence. In the Irish annals of the thirteenth century, the name is referred to as Kill Orglain, the Church of Orgla. Nearby is the ring fort, which has a souterrain. There are many other souterrains and raths in the vicinity.

Crossing the River Laune at Killorglin the traveller passes the Bianconi Inn and climbs the steep incline to the town square. Much of the town still possesses an atmosphere of bygone days, with some shops like Sheehan's and Dodd's maintaining their original facades. Like so many Kerry towns Killorglin is noted for its number and variety of pubs. I particularly recommend the Bianconi Inn which also serves good food. Beside the bridge the Fishery Restaurant and Craft Shop is worth a visit. Another place worth dropping into is the Basement Museum to see its historical artefacts and memorabilia. Bikes can also be hired in the town. For those with stamina, the time to visit Killorglin is during Puck Fair in August when drink is plentiful but sleep is scarce.

The town was originally held by the Moriartys until they were ousted in the eleventh century by McCarthy, King of Munster and the Anglo-Normans. Killorglin Castle, later to be known as Conway Castle, was built in 1215 by Geoffrey de Marisco. De Marisco established the Manor of Killorglin and brought the Augustinian monks to Killagha. Killorglin was to fall under their jurisdiction. De Marisco's grand-daughter, Christiana, inherited Killorglin Manor but sold it to Sir Maurice Fitzmaurice. In time the land came under the control of the Earl of Desmond.

Following the death of the Earl of Desmond in November 1583 and the killing of Fitzmaurice, the lands of the Earl and his allies became the property of the Crown and plans were made for the plantation of Munster. In 1587 the lands were granted to Jenkin Conway who was required to have English tenants on his estate. 'Grant to Captain Jenkin Conway, esq, of the castle and lands of Killorglin, in the counties of Kerry and Desmond, containing 1304 acres of which 476 are arable. To hold for ever, by the name of Castle Conwaie ... Grantee may impack eighty acres. He shall build houses for eighty acres. He shall build houses for eight families, of which one is to be for himself, one for a freeholder of eighty acres, and one for a farmer of eighty acres.'

Conway died in 1612 and was succeeded by his son, also Jenkin, and in 1613 James I confirmed his ownership of the territory. The first Blennerhassett, named Robert, with his aged father, Thomas, came to Ireland from Cumberland, as a planter), in the reign of Elizabeth I. He married Captain Conway's daughter, Elizabeth, from whom all the families of Blennerhassett in Kerry descended. A monument was erected opposite the Catholic church to the memory of Townsend Blennerhassett, a member of the Kerry Militia, who was drowned on 20 June 1867 while rescuing a friend. The family mansion of the Blennerhassetts was built in the eighteenth century on the site of the old Norman castle. An attempt was made in the district to introduce Protestantism in 1830, but it only alienated people and failed totally.

Myth and legend have surrounded Mount Laune (Cnocán Ard Dearg), a cone-shaped red hillock which was reputed to have connections with Fionn Mac Cumhail and the Fianna (a legendary warrior band). The Piper's Stone, a giant stone situated on Courauree Hill, was associated with a great piper, Sean O'Duibhgin, and stories of fairy music. Close to the river is the sixteenth-century tower of Murray Castle, Ballymalis.

In 1613 James I granted a patent 'to hold a fair in Killorglin on Lammas Day and the day after'. The following is a song about the Puck Fair written by John Purcell.

> All young lovers that are fond of sporting,
> Pay attention for a while,
> I will sing you the praises of Puck Fair,
> And I'm sure it will make you smile;
> When the lads and lassies coming gaily
> To Killorglin can be seen,
> To view the Puck upon the stage,
> As our hero dressed in green.
>
> And hurra for the gallant Puck so gay,
> For he is a splendid one:
> Wind and rain don't touch his tail,
> For his hair is thirty inches long.

The Puck Fair (Aonach an Phuic) is one of the country's foremost festivals. Originally held on Lammas Day (1 August), the fair is now held annually in mid-August. A male goat, known as puck, is captured in the Macgillycuddy Reeks and is enthroned for the three days of the fair on an elevated platform. On Gathering Day the puck is paraded through the streets before being hoisted aloft. Fair Day is given over to buying and selling cattle, horses and pigs. On Scattering Day the puck is ceremoniously released back to the mountains. Many travelling people and traders converge on the town for the occasion.

John Millington Synge in his book *In West Kerry* gave an account of the Fair. 'The greatest event in West Kerry is the horse-fair, known as Puck Fair. On the main roads, for many days past I have been falling in with tramps and trick characters of all kinds, sometimes single and sometimes in parties of four or five. Cavalcades of every sort were passing from the west with droves of horses, mares, jennets, foals and asses, with their owners going after them in flat or railed carts, or riding on ponies. Near the first public-house, blind beggars were kneeling on the pathway, praying with almost Oriental volubility for the souls of anyone who would throw them a coin.'

There are many stories as to the origins of the Puck Fair. One account tells how Cromwellian troops were camped at the foot of the Macgillycuddy Reeks. A herd of goats took fright before the invaders. One puck broke away from the herd and while they headed for the mountains, the one lone puck headed for Killorglin. The exhausted goat alerted the people to the approaching danger and the townspeople held a festival in his honour. Another version told of the sale of a single goat at an otherwise deserted fair. Other sources regarded it as being part of the solar festival of Lugh, the Celtic Sun-God of the Tuatha Dé Danann.

The first train of the Great Southern and Western Railway came to Killorglin on 15 January 1855. One unique feature of the railway network was the viaduct at Killorglin, known as the metal bridge. On 12 September 1893 this line was continued to Cahirciveen and Valentia Island. On 30 January 1960 this line closed, like so many other branch lines throughout the country. The old saw mill was built by the de Moley family in the late 1860s and the eight-arched stone bridge was constructed in 1885.

On Good Friday 1916 three Irish Volunteers taking part in the rebellion were drowned when their car took a wrong turn in the town and plunged off Ballykissane pier into the river. The men were travelling to the wireless college in Cahirciveen to take wireless equipment in an effort to signal Roger Casement and the *Aud*, the German arms ship. A monument was erected to the memory of the men, Con Keating, Charles Monahan and Donal Sheehan, on Ballykissane pier. In 1920 a detachment of Black and Tans burned the old mill and several other buildings in the town. During the Civil War, in the summer of 1922 the town was held by Republicans but by September Free State troops had taken and occupied the town. On 22 September a Republican force of five hundred led by Sean Hughes and Humphrey Murphy made an assault in an attempt to re-take the town but they failed to overwhelm the garrison of sixty men. They attempted to burn the barracks and other important buildings but the attack was a failure, with many Republican casualties.

RECOMMENDED

The Puck Fair, held in mid-August.

The River Laune, noted for its salmon and trout fishing.

Monument on Ballykissane Pier.

The stone bridge built in 1885.

Basement Museum.

Visitors' Information Centre.

Fishery Restaurant and Craft Shop near the bridge.

KILLORGLIN

Glenbeigh

The village of Glenbeigh is a tourist centre at the mouth of the River Beigh, which rises five miles to the south-west in the crag-surrounded loughs named Coomasaharn, Coomreagh and Coomacarra. It takes its name Gleann Beithe (Valley of the Beigh, or birch trees) from the river.

Following the main road westwards from Killorglin the traveller will reach Glenbeigh. Here you will be well rewarded for making a detour eastwards to the circular drive around Caragh Lake. The lake, in a tranquil setting, is noted for its salmon and trout fishing. Adjacent to the lake is Lickeen forest which is ideal for walkers. In fact one of Kerry's best known walks, the Kerry Way, extends from here. The tracks and roads lead across to the Macgillycuddy Reeks and to the highest mountain in Ireland, Carrantuohill, standing at 3,414 feet. This is always a challenge for dedicated climbers. Well worth a visit is Rossbeigh Beach which is ideal for swimming, surfing and leisurely strolls. Leaving the town on the Ring of Kerry road there are excellent views of Dingle Bay and the mountains on the Dingle peninsula. Close to the village on the Rossbeigh road is a forest trail which offers scenic views.

The area around Glenbeigh and Glencar is rich in legends of the Fianna. Diarmuid and Gráinne are reputed to have spent some time in a cave in Behy valley. Gráinne was betrothed to Fionn, leader of the Fianna but she eloped with a Kerryman, named Diarmuid Ó Duibhne. They took refuge in a cave near Glenbeigh but Fionn pursued them for seven years. The amphitheatre of mountains are named 'The Glenbeigh Horseshoe', in the Glen of the River Behy. In the vicinity, Cool Naharragill has a stone with concentric circles and other writings. At Laghtfinnan Penitential station, where pilgrims stopped to pray, there is a cairn and an ogham stone which is believed to mark the grave of St Fionán, patron of the parish.

In the late seventeenth century, an iron smelting works, which was developed by Sir William Petty after the Cromwellian conquest, operated in the foothills of Glencar. There was large-scale destruction of forests to supply fuel for the works. When Petty cleared the district of charcoal the works were forced to close.

A Mr Wales built an inn in 1830, which is now the Olde Glenbeigh Hotel. Glenbeigh was serviced by a new road linking it to Cahirciveen and Waterville. The area was badly affected during the famine period with widespread starvation. In 1798, the parish priest of Glenbeigh gave the Fenians his blessing as they headed for Killarney, but his brother, parish priest of Valentia Island, was extremely anti-Fenian. During the 1880s many tenants in the Glenbeigh area fell into arrears with their rents and there were widespread evictions.

In 1867 the fourth Baron Headley of Aghadoe assigned Lord Wynn to build Glenbeigh Towers, a castellated mansion which became known as Wynn's Folly. Headley was displeased with the results and took legal action against him. He fancied himself as a feudal baron and took initiatives to encourage the tourist trade. To relieve distress during the famine he built estate roads, reduced rents and permitted arrears to be paid in labour. Tenants who owed him a total of £5000 of arrears paid by their work in embanking five hundred acres against the sea. The fifth Lord Headley became a Muslim and was known as 'Al Hadji'. During the period of the Truce in 1922, several big houses in the area were burned, including Headley Towers.

Close to Glenbeigh is the four mile golden strand of Rossbeigh (Ros Beithe, the Peninsula of Birch Trees). In the nineteenth century a stone tower was built at the northern end of the beach as a marker for ships entering Castlemaine Harbour. The beach also featured in the mythology of the area. Fionn's son, Oisín is reputed to have ridden with Niamh on white horses along the beach at Rossbeigh and out over the waves to Tír na nÓg (the mythological Land of Youth).

A regular feature was the Rossbeigh Strand Races and John Millington Synge, who spent periods at Mountain Stage in the early 1900s, gave a colourful description of the event: 'The races had to be run between two tides while the sand was dry, so there was not much time to be lost, and before we reached the strand the horses had been brought together, ridden by young men in many variations of jockey dress. For the first race there was one genuine racehorse, very old and bony, and two or three young horses belonging to farmers in the neighbourhood. The start was made from the middle of the crowd at the near end of the strand, and the course led out along the edge of the sea to a post some distance away, back to the starting-point, round a post, and out and back once more.'

West of Glenbeigh is the picturesque area of Kells Bay, with another sandy beach, Cnoc na Tobar and its Stations of the Cross, dating from the Penal days. The Great Southern and Western Railway line ran through tunnels and over viaducts in this district en route to Cahirciveen and Valentia Island. South of the village is Glencar, (Gleann-an-Chairthe, the Glen of the Rock or pillar stone). Nearby Caragh Lake is a popular spot for salmon and trout fishing. The Fenian, John O'Neill Golden, was born at the Kerry Way, at Coomasaharn. He was transported (deported) to Australia after the Fenian Rising of 1867.

Glenbeigh Towers, or Wynn's Folly, Glenbeigh

RECOMMENDED

Dooks, 18 hole golf course.
Rossbeigh Beach.
Olde Glenbeigh Hotel.
Ruins of Glenbeigh Towers.
Cappanalea Outdoor
Education Centre.
Glenbeigh Riding Stables.
Wynn's Folly.
Glenbeigh Forest Walk.
Towers Hotel.

... EMBOSSED IN A BOLD MOUNTAINOUS COUNTRY ...

Cahirciveen

Old Dingle has true men, good sailors and oarsmen,
Kenmare ever proud of her sportsmen has been,
Waterville knows something of fox and hare hunting
But the hub of Old Ireland is Cahirciveen.

This claim may be something of an exaggeration but Cahirciveen (also spelt Caherciveen and Cahersiveen) is certainly the hub of the Iveragh Peninsula. The town is situated at the foot of Beentee Mountain, overlooking Valentia Island on the Fertha River. Its name in Irish, Cathair Saidhbhín, means Little Sadhbh's Fort. The name originated from a caher or fort near the old hospital, but the source of the name Saidhbhín (or Sabina) is unknown.

Following the main road from Glenbeigh will bring you to Cahirciveen, which is the largest town on the Ring of Kerry. A first impression is of a town which has seen better days. The town centres around a sleepy Main Street, with shop fronts here and there boarded up. Don't miss the O'Connell Memorial Church. Two places worth a browse are the Old Curiosity Shop and the Old Oratory Craft and Coffee Shop. A mile north of the town on the Glenbeigh side is Carhen House, the ruins of Daniel O'Connell's birthplace. The ruins of Ballycarbery Castle lie two miles west.

The area is rich in archaeological monuments and folklore. There are late Stone Age spirals on rock carvings over 5,000 years old, several standing stones, Celtic monastic settlements, souterrains and stone forts. There are three historic forts, Cahir-na-Cabal, Cahergele and Castlequinn. Cahergele, to the north of the castle, is a circular fort, similar to Staigue Fort, with stairs on the inside walls and the remains of a clochan. Northwest of the strand at Ballycarbery rises Doulus Head where Fionn Mac Cumhail and the Fianna are reputed to have fought some of their battles. Outside Cahirciveen is Knocknadober, on whose summit in pagan days the harvest festival of Lughnasa was celebrated. The mountain's holy well is dedicated to St Fursa and was once a place of pilgrimage.

Three miles north-west of Cahirciveen is Leacanabuaile Fort, a round stone fort with ten-foot-thick walls. Inside there are several stone beehive huts. The area was excavated in 1939 when bronze and iron objects were found, dating to the ninth or tenth century. A large stone ring fort, Cathair na gCat, is nearby. Across the estuary is Ballycarbery Castle, a stone fort built in the fifteenth century as a stronghold of the McCarthys. In 1652 the castle, then held by the O'Connells, was destroyed by Cromwellian forces under General Ludlow. Many colonists landed here and settled, bringing with them their respective cultures and customs.

The town originated around a road which was built at the end of the eighteenth century between Glenbeigh and Waterville. By 1815 there were only five houses with a small population. The quay and harbour were constructed in 1822 and development was rapid mainly through its farming community. Thirteen years later the population was over a thousand.

Warburton's *History of Dublin* of 1818 stated: 'the town of Caherciveen in the County Kerry, one hundred and sixty miles from Dublin, was thirty miles from the nearest post town, and so completely cut off from all communications with the metropolis, that, having some intercourse with America, the Dublin newspapers and letters used sometimes to arrive there via New York having twice crossed the Atlantic.' (In fact, this account underestimates the distance from Dublin to Cahirciveen.)

Cahirciveen did not impress Mr and Mrs S.C. Hall during their travels in 1865 and they wrote: 'We come in sight of Cahirciveen, this is the town of the district commanding the whole trade of the county within a circuit of nearly forty miles, north, south and east. Yet Caherciveen is little better than it was thirty years ago, a dull town, that conveys no idea of either activity or prosperity, although its advantages are large and many.'

The old police barracks beside Valentia River (below) is of a distinctive style of architecture. Apparently the plans for the barracks and another set for a fortress in India got mixed in transit and the incorrect buildings were constructed in each location!

The IRB had considerable support in the area and in February 1867 there was an attempt at revolution. It was the only Fenian rising in Kerry in 1867. They planned to take the barracks but the police were alerted and the plan was aborted. The English planned to capture O'Connor, leader of the Fenians and Colonel Curzon reported: 'Caherciveen I have seen and I have no hesitation in saying that I never saw so vile a spot . . . the appearance and the manner of the people of that place stamp it as a den of mischief.'

CAHERSIVEEN
CARHAN HSE (DAN. O'CONNELL)

Daniel O'Connell, known as the Liberator, spent his childhood in Carhen House, about a mile from the town, where he was born on 6 August 1775, eldest son of Morgan and Catherine O'Connell. The O'Connell Memorial Church was one of the only Catholic churches in the world dedicated to a layman. The church was built in the Main Street in 1888 in memory of O'Connell and was designed by George Ashlin. Canon Brosnan planned to build a church to commemorate the centenary of the Liberator's birth but the Bishop of Kerry and the Archbishop of Cashel would not grant him permission. In 1883 Canon Brosnan travelled to Rome and Pope Leo XIII gave him permission for his church and instructed Archbishop Croke to lay the foundation stone.

In 1888 Richard Lovett, the travel writer, wrote: 'Cahirciveen is a poor but apparently thriving little town. It lies embossed in a bold mountainous country. It is thirty-eight miles from Killarney, and few mail-car rides in Ireland so well repay the fatigue involved in their accomplishment.'

During the Civil War there was a good deal of activity in the area. The town was held throughout the summer of 1922 by Republicans but on 23 August that year a hundred Free State troops under Brigadier Tom O'Connor sailed to Valentia and took Cahirciveen. The barracks was destroyed and Commandant Lynch was shot dead. On 12 March 1923 five local men were tied to a landmine by soldiers and shot in the legs before the mine exploded. This was a reprisal for an earlier killing of Free State troops.

A branch line of the railway from Farranfore reached Cahirciveen in 1893 and the line closed in 1960. The Valentia Meteorological Station, a mile outside the town, is one of the most important weather stations on the western seaboard of Europe. At the inlet called Connorown, the cables from America come ashore, crossing thence to Valentia where they are visible at low tide.

Jack O'Shea, known affectionately as 'Jacko', one of the great players of the victorious Kerry football team of the 1970s and 1980s, was born in Cahirciveen. He won seven All-Ireland medals and six All-Star awards.

RECOMMENDED

The O'Connell Memorial Church.

Ruins of Ballycarbery Castle.

Monument to those killed in 1916.

The Old Curiosity Shop.

The Old Oratory Craft and Coffee Shop.

Ruins of Carhen House.

... HOUSES BRIGHTLY PAINTED AND REEKS OF TURF ...

Portmagee

Four miles from Cahirciveen is another well worthwhile detour. Leaving the main road, a signpost for Portmagee leads across flat bogland to Portmagee, a small fishing village on the Portmagee Channel which separates the southern coast of Valentia Island from the mainland. Portmagee (Port Mhig Aoidh, Magee's Harbour) is named after the widow of Captain Theobald Magee, who was an officer in King James' army at the Battle of the Boyne (1690). Following the battle Magee made his home here and sailed regularly between France, England and Ireland. After his death in 1727, his wife and children settled in what would thereafter become known as Port Magee.

Houses are brightly painted and reeks of turf are neatly stacked adjoining the pier. There is a seafood restaurant and a number of atmospheric pubs. At this juncture the channel is only 360 feet wide and a bridge connects Valentia Island to the mainland.

The village has long been associated with the sea — fishing, smuggling and shipwrecks. Most of the south west Kerry fishing fleet were based here. From here mail and supplies were brought to the lighthouse keepers on the Skelligs. In 1911 *The Lady Crompton*, en route from Buenos Aires to Liverpool, ran aground at Carraig. The crew, including some blacks, who intrigued the locals, climbed a cliff to safety. In recent years the anchor from *The Lady Crompton* was salvaged and put on display at Knightstown on Valentia Island.

Around the turn of the century there was good employment for women in gutting and salting mackerel and packing them into barrels for transportation to Dublin or export abroad. Despite its closeness to Valentia Island the only direct link was by ferry. Cattle, supplies and passengers had to be transported by boat. Curraghs were used mainly for sport out of Portmagee.

From 1911 numerous efforts were made to build a bridge linking Valentia to the mainland. Several plans and surveys were undertaken, until finally in 1955 Portmagee was chosen as the site. Work commenced in 1967 and the bridge opened to traffic in 1971.

There are many archaeological sites in the vicinity of the village such as Illaunloughan, St Loughan's Island, off Portmagee, with its shrine tomb, beehive hut and souterrain. West of Portmagee is Reencaheragh Castle, built in the twelfth century. It has two small guard cells and concealed caves. Nearby is Puffin Island, so called because of the birds inhabiting it.

RECOMMENDED

Reencaheragh Castle.
St Loughan's Island, with
shrine tomb and beehive
huts.

... THE EYE LINGERS WITH DELIGHT ...

Valentia Island

Valentia Island is linked to the Ring of Kerry by a road at Portmagee. The island, whose ancient name was Oileán Dairbhre (the Island of the Oak Woods), is a mere seven miles by three and has a population of six hundred, most of whom live by farming and fishing. A later name was Dairbhre Ó Duibhne (Oak Woods of the O'Duibhne) or Dairbhre (Place of the Oaks). From the fifteenth century the island became known as Valentia and there is speculation as to its origin from the Spanish province of Valencia, or the Irish, Béal Inse (Mouth of the Island, from the sound beside it). In summer the island is serviced by a passenger ferry at Renard Point. The island has two villages, Knightstown on the north shore and Chapeltown in the centre of the island's farmland. Valentia Harbour is deep and sheltered, but the entrance is narrow and is protected to the north by Beginish Island.

Crossing the bridge at Portmagee the traveller will turn back the clock to a bygone era. This is the ideal location for anyone seeking solitude and a walking or cycling holiday. The mildness of the climate means travellers will be able to spot palm trees and tropical plants. They will be enchanted by the smell of turf fires and a quiet pint and chat with locals. There are magnificent views of the Skelligs and the more distant Blasket Islands. The pier head at Knightstown is in a postcard setting with the pier, lightboat, fishing boats and the lighthouse. This is the best starting point for visiting the Skelligs and for hiring boats for deep sea angling. On the island there is a range of accommodation for tourists from self-catering to B&Bs to hostels, including An Óige and the Royal Pier Hostel. The traveller can learn more about island life by a visit to the Heritage Centre at Knightstown. A new amenity for tourists is the Skellig Experience and Visitor Centre which offers an audio-visual programme and exhibits of the early history of the island.

In 812 the Vikings attacked the island. The first of the Anglo-Normans to land on the island was Maurice Fitzgerald. Later Valentia became part of the lands of the MacCarthy Mór and one of the clan became known as Baron of Valentia. In 1620 Lord Anglesey was given the title Viscount Valentia by James I and was granted land on the island. Trinity College, Dublin, also received a grant of land on the island in the seventeenth century. Cromwell's Fort and a lighthouse stand on a headland called Fort Point, a reminder of the fact that the Protector erected forts at each end of the island in 1653 to protect the coast and to prevent pirate ships from using the island to evade the authorities. Another prominent castle was Ballycarbery Castle close to the harbour. During the Spanish and French wars the British fortified the forts and castle with cannon and Valentia became a strategic advance naval base. There is speculation that at least one of the ships of the Spanish Armada was wrecked off the island with three hundred men on board. There was no record of survivors. Many Spanish vessels used Valentia and traded in wines while agricultural produce, hides and wool were exported.

Most of the island belonged to the Knights of Kerry, descendants of Maurice Fitzgerald who resided at Glanleam House (the Glen of the Elms), the old name for the estate. He developed its farm and gardens which were situated in a densely wooded area, noted for its enormous fuchsias. In the early nineteenth century, Sir Peter Fitzgerald, Bart, the nineteenth Knight of Kerry, opened a slate quarry on the island and promoted its produce energetically in England. The quarry supplied slate for the Houses of Parliament in London. The slates were of old red sandstone and quarried from the side of a hill. The quarry failed because of lack of cheap transport as well as keen competition from Wales. It re-opened for a period in 1902 but never again flourished and was later turned into a religious grotto.

The first Trans-Atlantic cable was laid from Valentia and gave a great boost to employment on the island. Work commenced on the project on 5 August 1857 but six days later it snapped, after three hundred miles had been laid. A second attempt failed due to a violent storm on 20 June 1858. The third attempt was successful and on 5 August 1858, the first message passed between Queen Victoria and President Buchanan of the United States. On 4 September this cable also failed, after 271 messages had been transmitted. It was not until 1865 that another attempt was undertaken, but it snapped in mid-ocean. Another successful cable was laid in July 1866. The cable station finally closed in 1965 due to advances in communications. When the Fenians planned their abortive 1867 Rising they had hoped to broadcast news of the Rising from the island.

In 1880 Richard Lovett gave the following account of the island: 'The broad strait forming Valentia Harbour, the mountain, the many tones of brown on the hills, the clear sky, the fine colours of the water, combine to make this a scene upon which the eye lingers with delight. In the extreme left of the larger engraving a little cluster of houses is shown. This is the headquarters of the celebrated Atlantic Telegraph Company. The second building from the left is the house in which the instruments are kept busy day and night constantly receiving and transmitting messages across the Atlantic.'

The Government financed the extension of the railway from Killorglin to Valentia and construction work began in 1890. Although it was a service badly needed by the community it was a complex line to lay, as tunnels had to be dug and the tracks laid above cliffs. The cost of this section of the line was £8,800 per mile, and it opened a regular service on 12 September 1893. During the early years of the Second World War, large quantities of fish were landed at Valentia Harbour and transported by special trains to Dublin or Fishguard for shipment to England. Like so many other lines in the country, this branch line closed in 1960.

A watch tower was erected on Bray Head in 1815, situated above the steep cliffs which rise eight hundred feet above the sea. During 'the Emergency' (as World War Two was euphemistically known in Ireland!) the tower was occupied by coast watchers. Close by are the remains of several beehive huts. There are many holy wells on the island, the best known being St Brendan's. The small village of Knightstown is known locally as 'the foot' and in 1825 the Government gave a grant towards the construction of a pier there. West of the village are the remains of the medieval Kilmore church. Many British royalty visited Valentia. In 1869 Prince Arthur and his entourage were greeted warmly by the islanders. He gave permission for the hotel to be called 'The Royal Hotel' in his honour. In 1897 the Duke and Duchess of York toured the island.

On Easter Sunday 1916 the Killarney Volunteers were ordered to sever the cable between Valentia Island and Killarney and then to link up with the Castleisland Volunteers and move on to Newcastlewest. With the cancellation of orders the plan was abandoned. When the Rising commenced in Dublin, Tim Rice, an IRB man working in the cable station in Valentia, sent a coded message to John Devoy in New York. It read: 'Mother successfully operated on today.' Immediately Devoy rang London but they had not yet heard of the Rising. On Good Friday 1916 three Volunteers travelling to Valentia to signal the German arms ship, the *Aud*, were drowned when their car drove off the pier at Killorglin.

During the 1940s there was no secondary school on the island and children had to travel by ferry to Renard Point on the mainland and cycle from there to the Presentation Convent in Cahirciveen.

From the 1850s temperature and weather readings were taken on the island and a meteorological observatory was established there in 1867. In 1892 the observatory was moved to the mainland. Due to the island's westerly position the mean annual temperature is as high as 51°F and winters are exceptionally mild. The mild climate accounts for the myrtle, arbutus, ferns and other exotic tropical plants which grow in abundance. Flax has been grown extensively in the area.

Sport has always featured strongly in the lifestyle of the island. Mick O'Connell was born here on 4 January 1937 and spent most of his life, apart from a term studying engineering at University College Cork and a brief spell in England, on the island. In 1959 he became the first member of the local Young Islanders Club to win a senior All-Ireland medal with the Kerry team which he also captained that year. He later won All-Ireland medals in 1962, 1969 and 1970 and several National League titles with his native county.

RECOMMENDED

Slate Quarry and Grotto.
Royal Pier Hostel.
Valentia Heritage Centre.
Huge anchor from The
Lady Crompton.
Gallery Kitchen Restaurant.
The Boston Pub.
An Óige Hostel.
Valentia Diving Centre.
The Skellig Experience,
Visitor Centre and Cruise
to Skelligs.

... FOR A RENT OF TWO HAWKES AND PUFFIN FEATHERS ...

The Skelligs

The stout Amergin was in battle slain,
Ir lost his life upon the western main
Skellig's high cliffs the hero's bones contain;
In the same wreck Arranan too was lost.

This early reference to the Skelligs appeared in the old annals and told of the mythological figure, Ir, who was shipwrecked here during the Milesian invasion. A boat trip to Skellig Michael would be the highlight of a visit to the area. Choose a clear day to make the trip — and it's not suitable for those who suffer from vertigo! Alternatively, the Skellig Experience is a visitor centre on Valentia Island opposite Portmagee which provides information on the Skelligs and a cruise near the islands. To land on the Skelligs, take a trip on one of the local, privately-run boats.

The Skelligs (in Irish, na Scealga, the Splinters or, according to another source, Sceilig meaning Sea Rock), are situated nine miles south-west of Portmagee and consist of three rocky inlets, the Great Skellig, Little Skellig and Lemon Rock or Washerwoman's Rock. The Great Skellig is a sharp-pointed mass of rock, rising sheer from the Atlantic in twin peaks, 715 and 650 feet high, and ringed by high, almost inaccessible cliffs.

Notes of Irish Architecture by the Earl of Dunraven in 1875 quotes an ancient manuscript: 'This Rocke stands three leagues from the earth in the main ocean. It is at least 700 perches long and high, and with adoe one can climb up the stayres to it at a time. At the top of this rock is a church built, and a churchyard about it. It is named from the Archangell St Michael, in Irish Sceilig Mhichil, Schellig Michael.'

Tradition has it that a community of monks sailed from the mainland in skin boats to the island to seek a life of prayer and solitude. They built beehive huts and slept on stone beds, living on bread, herbs and spring water. The Skelligs were attacked and plundered by the Vikings in 823, leaving the monks to starve in their cells. Along with their booty the Vikings carried away Eitgal, Abbot of the Skelligs. The Annals of the Four Masters recorded the deaths of two Abbots of Skellig, Blathmac in 950 and Aodh in 1044. Legend has it that St Malachy was driven from Bangor and took refuge on Skellig Michael. The monastery was situated on narrow terraces.

In 1674 Charles II granted the Skelligs to the Countess of Mountrath. The islands were later acquired by the Butlers of Waterville for a rent of 'two hawkes and a quantitie of puffin feathers yearly.' Butler sold the Great Skellig to the Commissioners of Irish Lights for £800 and three lighthouses were built on it in succession. The lighthouse on the island, forty-six feet high and 175 feet above sea level, opened in 1865. The lighthouse keeper, his wife and children lived on the island. Boats sailed to the Skelligs from a number of nearby ports, including Portmagee and Cahirciveen.

Until late in the eighteenth century this was a celebrated place of pilgrimage to which people came to follow the way of the Cross. Charles Smith in his *History of County Kerry* stated that the Great Skellig 'had been visited by great numbers of people ever since the time of St Patrick by way of piety and devotion.' These rocky islands were also called, 'the most western of Christ's fortresses in the ancient world.' There is still evidence of the chapel, cells, burial grounds, a holy well and stone crosses. On the eastern side a series of steps mark the ascent of the main settlement. The approach today is by the lighthouse road. The Little Skellig is a noted breeding ground for gannet and thousands of them congregate on the island. Today, with the lighthouse run automatically, only the birds remain.

... A MAINLAND BASE AND STANDING STONES ...

Ballinskelligs

On returning to Portmagee the traveller can continue south over the 1100 foot Coomanaspig Pass, across the Glen to the quiet village of Ballinskelligs. Ballinskelligs is west of Waterville, off the Ring of Kerry Road. The name Ballinskelligs, Baile an Sceilg in Irish, means the Homestead or Townland of Skellig Island. The first Celtic invaders are reputed to have landed at Ballinskelligs. The road to Ballinskelligs offers magnificent views of St Finan's Bay, the Skelligs and Ballinskelligs Bay. The four-mile sandy beach is suitable for swimming. From Ballinskelligs pier you can take a boat out to the Skelligs or Puffin Island. Also worth a visit are the stained glass windows in St Michael's Church, which are from the Harry Clarke studios. In recent times, the Ballinskelligs area has become popular for holiday homes.

An early Christian monastic settlement was established at Kildreelig on the Bolus Road. They erected an oratory, two inscribed stones and several beehive huts. Some monks who could no longer endure the solitude of island life on the Great Skellig came to live here. At Kildreelig there is also an alignment of four standing stones, believed to be the burial place of the mythological Milesian leader, Erannan.

South-west of the village is Bolus Head, overlooking St Finan's Bay and the Skelligs. St Fionán Lobhar established a monastery at Rathkieran. Nearby is the Pagan's Grave, a collection of standing stones. Maolmorna was a pagan who attempted to kill St Fionán but was himself slain. In the twelfth century, Killemlagh Church was erected on the site. Wedge graves are situated at Coom and at Meelagulleen and St Michael's Well is close to the village.

A priory was established in Ballinskelligs by the Arroastian Canons of St Augustine, and it flourished until Elizabethan times when their lands were confiscated and granted to Robert Harding, a British merchant. Ballinskelligs Abbey, the Augustinian priory, was said to have been built at the end of the ninth century as a mainland base for the monastic settlement on the Skelligs. In 1569 the Crown ordered that an army garrison should be stationed in the Abbey. In the sixteenth century the McCarthy Castle was built at Ballinskelligs Point to defend the property against pirates and other invaders from the sea.

Kildreelig was a traditional Irish village with a thriving community. By the mid 1850s it had been devastated by famine and emigration to America. Plans are now in motion to revive the ancient village as an artists' retreat.

RECOMMENDED

Monastic settlement on Bolus Road.
Long sandy beach.
Remains of castle.
Windows in St Michael's Church which are from the Harry Clarke studio

... AT THE LITTLE WHIRLPOOL, A CONTINENTAL AIR ...

Waterville

From Ballinskelligs, return to the main Ring of Kerry road and turn right towards Waterville. The village of Waterville nestles between Lough Currane and the sea. Originally known as Bóthar an Coireáin (the Road of the Whirlpool or the Little Whirlpool), the village's English name was given to it by the Butler family. The whirlpool is in front of the Waterville Hotel where the Currane joins the Finglas River.

It is an exceptionally quiet village in winter, mainly dependent on the tourist trade. The village has a continental air with palm trees on the park beside the sea. I would particularly recommend the Butler Arms Hotel, Mick O'Dwyer's pub and restaurant and Sheilin Seafood Restaurant. Many shop signs are in Irish. A visit to O'Reilly's Post Office will revive memories of a bygone age. The post office is combined with an old style drapery shop with goods displayed in open boxes. Denis Donnelly's Tailor Shop is also worth a visit. Denis has conducted his trade here for over half a century and enjoys company.

Like much of South Kerry the area is rich in archaeological and early Irish mythological history. Above Lough Currane in the townland of Eightercua (Íochtar Cua: the Lower Hollow) are four gallauns or pillar stones, standing six to ten feet high and a stone circle, forty-five feet in diameter. There are many stories that the Milesians landed here and several burial places are said to date from that period. A Milesian legend relates that Lughnead, son of Ith, was drowned at Inbher Scene. Scene, wife of Amergin the Milesian poet, was drowned in Kenmare River and was buried at Eightercua. Close to the circle is the ancient church of Templenakilla. Within a mile radius there are other circles and gallauns. A dolmen at Ballybrack is said to be the burial place of another Milesian.

On Lough Currane is Church Island with St Fionán Cam's sixth-century church. It has three clochans and a monastery, supposedly founded by the twelfth-century reformer St Malachy following his expulsion from Bangor. South of Lough Currane the McCarthys had a stronghold where they fought the Anglo-Normans in the thirteenth century. The Butler family were appointed customs and excise officers in an attempt to stem the extensive smuggling along the coast. They were also granted the fishing rights on Lough Currane. The area became a popular angler's retreat with an abundance of salmon and trout. Shooting rights also became available for grouse, duck, cock, snipe and plover. Waterville House became the eighteenth-century residence of the Butler family. At Spunkane, near Waterville, Austin Stack addressed a large meeting in July 1917, urging those present to join Sinn Féin. On 25 August 1922 troops under Brigadier Tom O'Connor took Waterville.

For many years in his later life the renowned actor and director, Charlie Chaplin, and his family spent their holidays at the Butler Arms Hotel. They became popular figures locally, enjoying the fishing and walking. Waterville has an eighteen hole golf course, one of the longest in the world, on which many prominent figures including Bob Hope, Jack Nicklaus, Jack Lemmon, Sam Snead and Tony Jacklin have played. The village is also the home of the legendary Mick O'Dwyer, trainer of the victorious Kerry football team of the 1970s and 1980s. He first played senior football with the Waterville team in

RECOMMENDED

Waterville Leisure Centre.

*Waterville Lake Golf
Course, 18 holes.*

*Mick O'Dwyer's Pub and
Restaurant.*

Butler Arms Hotel.

Waterville Craft Market.

Donnelly's Tailor's Shop.

*The Huntsman Restaurant
and apartments.*

1950 when he was only fourteen. He won twelve Munster senior championship medals and four All-Ireland medals. As manager of the Kerry team from 1974, he led them to eight All-Ireland victories in a twelve-year period.

Above: Aerial view of Killarney (courtesy of Bord Fáilte), *Below:* Aghadoe (Jan de Fouw),
Overleaf: Beach at Cloghane (Remco de Fouw), *Inset left:* Knightstown, Valentia Island (Jan de Fouw),
Inset centre: near Ballinskelligs Bay (Jan de Fouw), *Inset right:* Dinglemen (courtesy of Bord Fáilte)

Cummeenduff (Jan de Fouw)

... A STONE FORT AND OAK WOOD ...

Caherdaniel

The village of Caherdaniel takes its name from a nearby pre-Christian fort or caher, Cathair Dónaill, Donal's Stone Fort, on the side of Tully Mountain. The caher is of a similar type and age as the Staigue Fort, with a simpler design but with no cells within the thickness of the walls. The caher was used as a pound until 1851.

This picturesque small village, with a mere handful of a population, is situated on a windy road above Derrynane Bay. There are several good viewing points along this road and it is advisable to pull in and explore the coastline. Allow time to visit Derrynane House, the home of Daniel O'Connell. The house is now a museum and open to the public. Foley's Bar is a good place for a light meal or drink.

Derrynane, meaning 'Fionan's Oak Wood', was situated amongst three hundred acres of bog and forest. The house was built by Captain John O'Connell in the early 1700s. The main part of the house was built by Donal Mór (grandfather of Daniel) in the mid eighteenth century, the first slated house in south Kerry. In the grounds there are smugglers' caves where contraband was concealed and from where men on the run sailed to the continent. Nearby is the Mass Rock where people worshipped during penal days. The estate's tenants lived in cabins close to the sea. The house also became a hunter's lodge for sportsmen and races were regularly held on the beach.

Daniel O'Connell, the eldest son of Morgan and Catherine O'Connell, was born in 1775 in Carhen, close to Caherciveen but his uncle Maurice, nicknamed 'Hunting Cap', adopted Daniel and his brother and took them to live in Derrynane House, on the northern shore of Kenmare estuary. Young Dan was to spend more time here as a child than at Carhen. His early education was from the parish priest and a local teacher before going to France for further education. Later when 'the Liberator', as he was known, married and began his political career he regularly spent time at Derrynane, fishing, hunting and beagling. He organised rallies and in 1829 he successfully achieved Catholic emancipation. Two years later he inherited Derrynane and despite the journey to London, which could take up to ten days to complete, he continually returned to Caherdaniel. He held meetings with colleagues in the morning on the lawn in front of the house. He defended the poor in corrupt courts and became the first Irish Catholic to take a seat in the British Parliament. Derrynane became the burial-place of the O'Connells, although Daniel was buried in Glasnevin Cemetery, Dublin. His often quoted last words were 'Send my heart to Rome and my body to Ireland.' In commemoration of the part played by O'Connell in securing Catholic emancipation, Derrynane has now been acquired as a national monument.

Aghavore Abbey on the nearby Abbey Island is reputed to have been built by St Fionán in the sixth century. Around the twelfth century the Augustinian canons occupied the friary. At high tide the Abbey is completely surrounded by water.

Kilcrohane church (St Criomthann's) built on Coad Mountain gave its name to the parish. Following the death of the parish priest, Fr Owen O'Sullivan, in 1784 the Civil Parish of Kilcrohane was divided into two

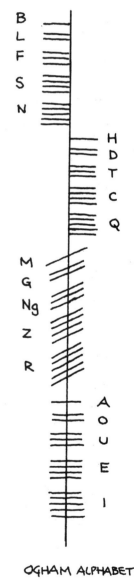

OGHAM ALPHABET

RECOMMENDED

*The Catholic Church is
worth a visit.*

*Derrynane House, home of
Daniel O'Connell. Open
all year.*

*Derrynane Hotel,
Caherdaniel.*

*Skellig Aquatics, Diving
Centre.*

*Derrynane Sea Sports
Centre.*

*Daniel O'Connell
Association Workshop held
in Derrynane Hotel in
October.*

Foley's Bar.

sections — Kilcrohane West, known as Caherdaniel or Bordoneen, and Kilcrohane East, known as Sneem or Ballybog. The O'Connell family built a new church in 1825. In the early 1800s Thomas Rua O'Sullivan, who wrote songs and poems in praise of Daniel O'Connell and wrote the famous 'Amhrán na Leabhar', had a row with the parish priest when a rival teacher arrived from Valentia Island. By the end of the nineteenth century the national schools in Caherdaniel Parish were Bunaneer Boys and Girls, Caherdaniel Boys and Girls, Farraniaragh, Glenmore and Lohar.

Below: Derrynane House, and facing page: Staigue Fort

Castlecove

STAIGUE FORT

The small coastal village of Castlecove is east of Caherdaniel, off the Ring of Kerry Road. Castlecove or Bunaneer was a square castle on the Kenmare River. Buninhar was a sixteenth-century tower house whose roof sloped to the ground, a mile north-east of the village. Close to the village, which takes its name from a small harbour, an ogham stone was transferred from its position below the water line to safety inland.

This is just a small village but a detour up a boreen to the left is a must. The traveller following a track to the head of an isolated valley will be truly rewarded by discovering Staigue Fort between two streams.

Staigue Fort (Cathair na Staige, the Stone Fort of the Bleak Place), is a circular building of massive stones, built with stone from the district. No exact date exists for the fort's origin but it is believed to be at least two thousand years old. It is generally accepted as belonging to the late Bronze or early Iron age. Tradition has it that the fort was built over the course of one day and one night. The women are said to have carried the stones in their skirts while the men did the construction. The building is about ninety feet in diameter, its dry stone walls thirteen feet at the base with a single entrance. It was used as a pound until 1790. Sheep now graze peacefully around this important site. Returning to the main road, a right turn will take you to a small harbour. Beside the Catholic Church is Staigue Fort Pottery and the traveller's thirst can be quenched in An Siopa Dubh.

One woman with a long association with Castlecove was the Honourable Albinia Lucy Broderick, an English aristocrat and sister of Lord Midleton, known affectionately as 'Lucy Broderick'. She trained as a nurse and in her early forties, around 1907, she left England for Kerry and began a campaign of helping and nursing the poor and needy. She learned the Irish language and

became a firm Republican. She began fund-raising in the hope of building a hospital but the project did not materialise. Following the War of Independence she became an ambulance driver. She lived amongst the locals almost as one of themselves.

RECOMMENDED

Staigue Fort.
Staigue Fort Pottery.

. . . SQUARES, TRIANGLES, PYRAMIDS AND BEEHIVE HUTS . . .

Sneem

The village of Sneem on the Ring of Kerry is situated on either side of the River Sneem. There are several interpretations of the name Sneem (An tSnaidhm, the Knot). One suggestion was that the name came from the winding river and the many roads which meet at that junction. A second was that it derived its name from the village's two squares. Another theory was that two trees grew facing each other on opposite banks of the river and they knotted together, forming a bridge.

This is my favourite village in the entire county. Its picturesque setting is enhanced by two squares, divided by a bridge, and the villagers must be congratulated on its appearance. Annually every house, pub and shop is painted a vivid colour. The village is litter free and the grass verges are always trimmed. Its cheerful appearance was recognised in 1987 when it won the Tidy Towns Competition. A new project beside the Catholic Church, nick-named 'The Pyramids' by locals, is worth a visit. It consists of a number of sculptures combining shapes of pyramids and beehive huts. A great place to stop for a coffee break, Sneem has several coffee shops, and the nearby Parknasilla Great Southern Hotel is noted for its afternoon tea. On leaving Sneem, detour at a signpost indicating Brushwood Studios Gallery. Follow the forest trail until you reach the gallery which has an amazing range of paintings, sculptures and batiks.

Sneem is noted for its two squares, referred to as north and south, though they are not squares but triangles, not north and south but east and west! On maps of the late eighteenth century the village of Sneem is referred to as 'Blandford', the Bland family being large land owners in the district. The first Bland came to Ireland in 1692 as chaplain to Lord Deputy Sidney. He became Vicar of Killarney and later acquired forfeited estates in Kerry including some in Sneem. Derryquin Castle was built as the family residence, close to the village.

In the estuary, two miles down from Sneem, lies the Earl of Dunraven's Garinish Island. Garinis (the Near Island) is full of exquisite plants. When the third Earl of Dunraven, a convert to Catholicism, witnessed the dire conditions in which the parishioners had to worship he built a new Catholic church, St Michael's, in Italian style in 1865 at his own expense. The first parish priest of the new independent parish of Sneem was Fr Joseph Power.

*Above: 'The Pyramids' and,
left: the Catholic Church, Sneem*

Fr Michael Walsh, parish priest of Sneem from 1829 to 1866, was a lover of Irish music and became the 'Fr O'Flynn' of the celebrated song by Alfred Perceval Graves.

Of priests we can offer a charmin' variety,
Far renowned for larnin' and piety;
Still, I'd advance ye without impropriety
Father O'Flynn as the pride of them all.

Alfred Perceval Graves, father of the distinguished author Robert Graves of *I Claudius* fame, spent some of his childhood here, swimming, fishing and exploring the islands. Another of the Graves family, Charles Graves, Protestant

Bishop of Limerick, once lived at what is now the Great Southern Hotel, Parknasilla. The Church of Ireland Church of the Transfiguration was built in 1810 and displays a salmon as a weathercock, above its tower.

In the early 1800s the roads were primitive and carriages found great difficulty making the journey from the outlying towns. By the late 1830s a new road had been constructed linking Sneem directly to Killarney and there was rapid development of the area. A Penny Post to Kenmare was initiated and Petty Sessions were held once a month. Fairs were held seven times a year for cattle, flannel and frieze. There was also a dispensary, an RIC barracks, two churches and two schools.

In 1841 the population of Sneem stood at 217, living in forty-seven houses. Two decades later the population was 406, in sixty-nine houses. The houses varied in size, from the mud cabins for the peasants to the big houses which were mainly south-east of the village. The gentry chose this location because of its sheltered position in Kenmare Bay and for its excellent fishing and hunting. The big houses in the Sneem area were Drimina, Reennafurrira, Hollywood, Askive, Derryquin, Glashnacree, Rossdohan and Parknasilla. The Church of Ireland congregation increased considerably when these houses were occupied.

The Presentation Sisters opened a convent in Sneem but it was not a success and they were forced to return to the mother house in Castleisland in 1891. A chapel of ease was built at Tahilla Bridge in 1873.

Many people believe Tahilla and Parknasilla to be villages in their own right, but the former is a mere cluster of houses and the latter the estate and forests surrounding the Great Southern Hotel. Parknasilla, Páirc-na-Saille (the Field of the Willows), was originally Derryquin Castle, the largest of the big houses, built by the Bland family in the 1860s. The property was leased to Rev Charles Graves, Bishop of Limerick in 1891 and four years later was taken over by the Southern Hotel. At the turn of the century a new hotel was opened which became the Great Southern Hotel. Many distinguished visitors stayed at the hotel including Prince Rainier and Princess Grace of Monaco in 1961 and President Charles de Gaulle in 1969. The man most associated with the hotel is George Bernard Shaw who found the setting most conducive for writing and completed most of *Saint Joan* while living there. The hotel has paid tribute to him with such names as the Shaw Library, Doolittle Bar and the Pygmalion Restaurant.

Several of the big houses were burned during the Civil War in 1922 including Askive, Derryquin Castle and Rossdohan House. A Royal Navy destroyer came into the bay, rescued some of the occupants and took them to safety in Cork whence they made their way to England.

The fifth President of Ireland, Cearbhaill Ó Dálaigh, had strong links with the area. Having resigned from the Presidency under controversial circumstances in 1976, he retired to Sneem with his wife. He died on 21 March 1978 and was buried in Sneem Cemetery. A sculpture was erected to his memory in the south square in 1983.

Other places of interest in the locality include Dukills Fort, a ring-fort a mile from Tahilla Bridge.

RECOMMENDED

Roman Catholic church.
Church of Ireland church.
The Pyramids.
Museum.
Brushwood Studios Gallery.
Peaceful Panda Sculpture in square.
Cearbhaill Ó Dálaigh Monument.

... A MODEL MARKET TOWN WITH ANCIENT STONES AND WELLS ...

Kenmare

The town of Kenmare (An Neidín, the Little Nest) is beautifully situated where the River Roughty flows into the estuary of the Kenmare River. In 1576 there was a reference to the town as Kenymarrie, Ceann Mara (The Head of the Sea, i.e. the highest point in a river reached by the tide). The area had extensive natural woodlands and, like so many other parts of the county, a fair share of ancient stones and wells. The Druid's Circle or Giant's Stone, over 3,000 years old, is south west of the town — a few minutes walk only — at Parknagullane and has fifteen standing stones, forming a circle about fifty feet in diameter. A larger stone stands in the centre. The monument is most likely a prehistoric burial place or a place of ritual assembly.

Close to Sheen Bridge was an early Christian church associated with St Finian the Leper. Our Lady's Holy Well and shrine at Gortamullen, known for its healing powers, is still a place of devotion.

Kenmare is a charming small town with a relaxed atmosphere giving the appearance of being well planned and prosperous. The town caters for a more affluent tourist than Killarney with two quality hotels, the Park and the Sheen Falls, and several good restaurants. I would suggest dropping into Micky Ned's for some of the most appetising sandwiches in Kerry. Quill's Woollen Market is the ideal venue for those seeking woollen goods and knitwear. A point of interest about the town is that the Church of Ireland rector is an American and has a congregation of only forty-eight. During the summer months there are guided tours around the town's historical sites. Recently Kenmare was selected as Kerry's representative for the Heritage Town Project.

On 20 July 1261 Finín McCarthy stopped an Anglo-Norman force at the Battle of Callan, close to the junction of the Rivers Slaheny and Roughty. Two Kerry Norman knights, John Fitzgerald and his son, Maurice (ancestors of the Earl of Desmond) were killed in the battle, leaving a baby named Thomas as heir. In the 1590s the parish of Kenmare was in the hands of three minor septs of the McCarthys. The Tuosist area was held by a sept of O'Sullivan Beare. Dunkerron Castle was built on a high rock in 1596 and became a stronghold of the O'Sullivan Mór.

The Cromwellian Government confiscated these lands from the Irish and they came into the possession of Sir William Petty. Petty had been assigned by the British Government to undertake the first systematic mapping of the entire country. What was to become known as the Down Survey (because it was the first survey of Ireland put down on paper) was successfully undertaken by Petty and as a reward the Government knighted him and presented him with 3,500 acres in Kenmare. In 1670 Petty established the town and brought in eight hundred English, Welsh and Cornish Protestant settlers. He developed an ironworks, lead-mines and a marble quarry which meant the widespread destruction of forests and a fishery along Kenmare Bay. Not long after Petty's death in 1687 the natives rebelled and 3,000 men laid siege to the town. The planters, under Richard Orpen, Petty's agent, resisted and took refuge in the White House but were outnumbered. Despite the odds the planters withheld a siege for five months and finally were allowed safe passage down the Kenmare River and safely reached Bristol. Petty's descendant, the Marquis of Lansdowne, and Trinity College, Dublin became the joint owners of the parish of Kenmare. Queen Elizabeth I granted a charter of land to the college.

Writing in *A Tour of Ireland* in 1779 Arthur Young recorded that 'Nedeen is a little town, very well situated, on the noble River Kenmare where ships of a hundred and fifty tons may come up. There are but three or four good houses. Lord Shelbourne, to whom the place belongs, has built one for his agent. There is a vale of good land, which is here from a mile and a half to a mile broad; and to the north and south, great ridges of mountains said to be full of mines.' He went on, 'Lord Shelbourne has a plan for improving Nedeen, to which he has given the name Kenmare, from his friend the nobleman, with that title, which, when executed, must be of considerable importance. It is to build ten cabins, and annex ten acres to each cabin, rent free for 21 years.'

Two other travellers, De Latocnaye in *A Frenchman's Walk Through Ireland* in 1796–97 and William Makepeace Thackeray in the nineteenth century, referred to Kenmare as 'a miserable little place'. There was a long tradition of liberal landlordism and moderate rents amongst the Catholic Earls of Kenmare. Early in the 1800s an inn and market house were erected in the town. The latter was used for the sale of local farming produce.

As a result of the famine many local people died and others sought refuge in the Kenmare Union Workhouse. The expense of maintaining the workhouse was deemed so excessive by the authorities that it was decided to provide some able-bodied paupers with the passage money to emigrate to the United States. On 25 February 1851 four cartloads of paupers left the workhouse on the first leg of their journey to Boston.

In September 1859 three sisters from the mother house of the Presentation Order from Castleisland opened a convent and school in Kenmare. For two years the work of the sisters progressed satisfactorily until the parish priest requested them to make changes in their rules. They were not to rise until 6 am and were not to commence school until 10. The nuns objected to these changes and as the parish priest would not yield they had no choice but to return to Castleisland in October 1861. The Poor Clare Sisters arrived in the town in 1861 and opened a convent adjoining the church. They were more

Above: Quill's Woollen Market, and left: Cromwell's Bridge, Kenmare

fortunate and had a long association with the town. They established a small lace-making industry to give employment to young local girls. Within a decade, Kenmare Lace had gained quite a reputation and at the Cork Exhibition of 1883 it won many awards. One of the nuns, Sister Mary Francis Clare Cusack, wrote many books including *History of Kerry* in 1871. In 1889 she published her candid autobiography entitled *The Nun of Kenmare*. The Holy Cross Catholic Church was built in 1864 by Fr J. O'Sullivan. The building was designed by Charles Hanson, son-in-law and one time partner of the eminent architect Augustus Welby Pugin.

By the end of the nineteenth century Kenmare was well catered for with a variety of transport. A stagecoach service connected the town with Killarney, Glengarriff and Bantry. Each week a Clyde Shipping Company Steamer called into Kenmare Pier. There was a lucrative export trade of wood to Wales and an importation of coal. In 1838 the first suspension bridge in Ireland was built over the Kenmare River at the expense of the first Marquis of Lansdowne, by Sir J. Brown, who was associated with the building of Brighton Pier. The Lansdowne house in Kerry was Derreen House, overlooking Kilmakilloge Harbour. In 1867 it was leased to J.A. Froude, author of *The English in Ireland* and *The Two Chiefs of Dunboy*.

The greatest improvement to the area was the introduction of a railway branch line from Headford Junction in September 1893. The Government provided finance to build branch lines, making travel more accessible to the remotest areas. Lord Lansdowne gave a grant of land through which the railway could run, free of charge. He also donated the Kenmare Station, known as Back Demesne. Following the opening of the railway and an increase in tourism, the Great Southern and Western Railway Company opened the Great Southern Hotel (now Park Hotel). During a visit to the town in 1903 King Edward VII dined at the hotel. On 31 December 1959 the railway line to Kenmare was closed.

On 21 March 1921 thirty British soldiers from Kenmare were fired on by the IRA at Headford Junction while waiting for a train to Killarney. Twenty-six of the soldiers were wounded and their attackers fled when reinforcements arrived. On 11 August 1922 two small ships from Limerick with 200 Free State troops under Commandant Scarteen O'Connor landed unopposed in Kenmare. The Republicans abandoned the town and took refuge in the mountains. On 9 September the Republicans attacked the town and shot O'Connor and his brother in their shop. The Republicans under John Joe Rice captured 110 rifles and 20,000 rounds of ammunition and held the town until Christmas.

In 1932 the suspension bridge spanning the Kenmare River was decreed unsafe and a new bridge was erected.

RECOMMENDED

Stone Circle.

Cappanacuss Castle, two miles west of town.

Convent of Poor Clares (lace display).

Walking Festival at Easter.

Golf Course, 9 Holes.

Ruins of St Finian the Leper Church.

Sheen Falls.

Park Hotel.

Sheen Falls Hotel.

Quill's Woollen Market.

Killarney and its Environs

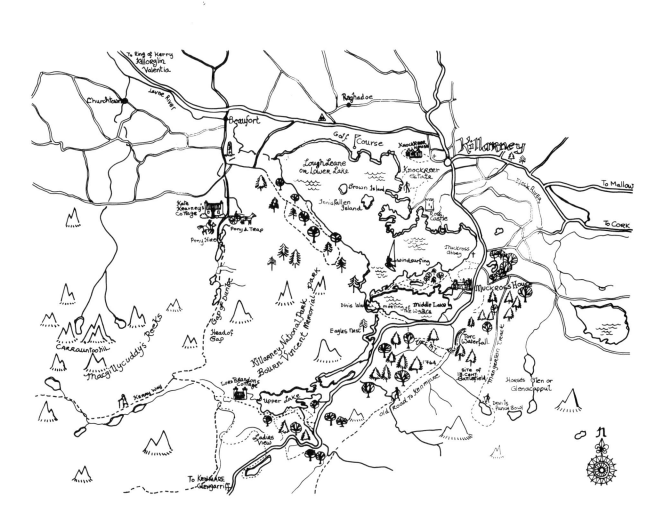

Killarney

By Killarney's lakes and fells,
Emerald isles and winding bays,
Mountain paths and woodland dells
Memory ever fondly strays
Bounteous Nature loves all lands,
Beauty wanders everywhere,
Footprints leaves on many strands,
But her home is surely there.
Angels fold their wings and rest
In that Eden of the West
Beauty's Home, Killarney,
Heaven's Reflex, Killarney. (Michael Balfe)

Killarney, in Irish, Cill Áirine or Cill Airne, meaning the Church of Airne, is called after a local holy man. Another interpretation was the Church of the Sloes. There is also a legend that three sister saints established themselves in this neighbourhood, and built churches there: their names were Aha, hence Kill-aha; Agi, hence Kill-agi; and Airne, hence Kill-airne. It became famous as a place of learning and piety.

Killarney is one of the most popular tourist centres in the entire country but when travellers first encounter the town, with its congested long main street full of pubs, drapery shops and newsagents, they might be forgiven for wondering if they have been misled or have misread their guidebooks. There is only a small number of buildings of architectural significance. Do not despair because on leaving the confines of the town and driving some miles out on the Muckross Road you will enter Killarney National Park and experience the true beauty of the area.

The area is most notable for its world-famous lakes, combined with its rugged beauty of valleys, mountains and its extraordinary wealth of trees and rare flowering-plants. There are three lakes, the Upper, the Middle or Muckross Lake, and the Lower or Loch Leane. The Upper and Middle Lakes are connected by a stream, the Long Range, ending in the rapids under the Old Weir Bridge. One of the most familiar sights today is that of the jaunting cars with American tourists enthralled by jarveys' tales of Kate Kearney's Cottage and the Gap of Dunloe.

Regardless of the weather, travellers will find plenty to occupy their time in Killarney. There are so many places of interest in the vicinity that I would require a full book to do them all justice. I will merely make a selection of my personal choices. At least one day should be allowed for exploring Muckross House and gardens and the walks around the lakes. The best time to see the rhododendron in full bloom is during May and June. Four miles from the town on the main road to Kenmare is Torc Waterfall. Eight miles further on is Lady's View which offers a magnificent view of the Upper Lake. Ross Castle is also worth a visit and beside the castle, tourists can take a trip on the lake by waterbus or rowing boat. Two and a half miles north west of the town are the ruins of Aghadoe church and round tower. The National Museum of Irish Transport should be of interest to all car lovers.

Killarney is the main tourist centre of the region and caters commercially for the needs of visitors, with Irish knitwear shops, traditional music, drives around the lakes by pony and trap and 'Irish nights' in hotels. The town boasts many top class hotels including the Great Southern, the Hotel Europe and Three Lakes. Lakelands Cottages, off Muckross Road offer 'away from it all' breaks.

In 1642 it was alleged that a number of Protestants were killed locally by the Irish. One of the best known of the Ferriter family, Piaras, a poet and rebel, was hanged by the Cromwellians in Killarney in 1653.

The fortunes of Killarney were closely linked with the Catholic Browne family who were ancestors of the Earl of Kenmare. Kenmare was the proprietor of the town and a large portion of the adjoining district. His family first entered Ireland in 1555 and his ancestor, Sir William Browne, received a

grant of 6,500 acres of the estates fortified in the Desmond rebellion. He increased this property by further purchases and by inter-marriage with the families of the Fitzgeralds, McCarthys and O'Sullivans.

When Sir William Petty completed his survey in 1656 there was a parish of Killarney, but no town or village of that name. In 1747, Killarney was no more than a scattered village, consisting of his Lordship's house, and not more than four slated houses and a hundred thatched cabins with a population of five hundred, centred around St Mary's Church of Ireland Church, which occupied the site of the original Church of Cill Airne.

The person actually credited with establishing the town was the fourth Viscount Kenmare, who developed the area around the church by building long narrow streets including New Street, Main Street and High Street. At the southern end of High Street the Kenmare family built Kenmare House in 1721 (having moved from Ross Castle). Another feature of Browne's plan was to initiate the development of the tourist industry by building hotels, inns, roads and boating and fishing facilities on the lakes. By the beginning of the nineteenth century the Brownes, from a base in Killarney, controlled a huge estate of 136,000 acres, stretching outwards from Kerry into Cork and Limerick. The Brownes remained true to the Catholic faith throughout this period.

Ross Castle, overlooking Lough Leane, was a sixteenth-century military stronghold of the O'Donoghue Clan. The castle was thought to be impregnable by land but Cromwell's General Ludlow brought in 1,500 troops in a fleet of flat-bottomed boats (built in Kinsale) up the River Laune which connected the lakes with the sea. The castle was held by Lord Muskerry and on seeing the fleet approaching he surrendered immediately. In 1652, it became the last castle in Kerry to fall to Cromwell's forces. The following year a number of those opposed to Cromwell's rule were hanged in Killarney. Nearby is O'Donoghue's Prison — an island of limestone rock on the lake which was used by the O'Donoghue chiefs to imprison rebels. In the winter of 1690 Major-General Tettau, a Dane, led an attack against the Irish in Kerry. The Irish retreated before him, burning the countryside en route until they reached Killarney. They sought shelter in Ross Castle which Tettau could not take as he had no heavy guns or mortars. Support from County Limerick was not forthcoming as they found the road impossible to pass. Tettau took a small fort near Ross Castle and killed the garrison, but bad weather and scarcity of supplies forced him to withdraw from Kerry, with little to show for his expedition.

At Aghadoe, on an elevated hill some miles from the town, are the remains of a sixth or seventh century monastic settlement, dedicated to St Fionán. In the eleventh century, O'Cathail, heir to the Kingdom of Loch Léin, was taken captive and killed. Around the same period a round tower and church were built here. The church was to become the arch-deanery of the diocese of Ardfert. Only the stump of the round tower remains.

In the 1780s, the Catholic bishops took up residence in Killarney. The Catholic Cathedral was designed by the eminent architect Augustus Welby Pugin and the foundation stone was laid in 1842, but the famine halted building in 1848. The cathedral was finally completed in 1855 and in later years it was extended and the spire added. In 1860 Bishop Moriarty invited Belgian friars to settle in the town. They came to a small house in Kenmare Place and finally the Franciscan Friary on Martyr's Hill or Gallows Hill was

built. St Mary's Church of Ireland Church was built in 1870 on the site of a fifteenth-century church which may have been the site of the original Cill Áirne.

To cater for the many destitute living in hovels in the vicinity it was necessary to open a workhouse in the 1850s. The inmates were accommodated in wards and dormitories and were given menial chores like grinding flour. Close to Torc waterfall is a spot where Kenmare men handed over the coffins of their dead to Muckross men in the 1850s to be interred in the Friary graveyard. Muckross people felt that this was their territory and would not allow Kenmare people to hold funerals there. Around this period there were frequent faction fights between the Moynihan and O'Donoghue families. Robert Emmet's mother, Elizabeth Mason, was born in Killarney and Emmet maintained close links with his relatives in Kerry.

Several visitors to the town gave their assessment of it. In 1812 Isaac Weld gave an account of three hundred slated houses and a population of approximately four thousand. Samuel Lewis gave an account in 1837 of brewing, milling and the manufacture of bandle linen as the town's chief industries. To foster the linen industry the fourth Viscount Kenmare brought in weavers from Northern Ireland. In the census of 1841 the population had reached seven thousand. In 1864 the travel writers Mr & Mrs S.C. Hall wrote in 'Killarney and the South of Ireland': 'The town of Killarney is a poor town;

and although surrounded by resident gentry can scarcely be described as prosperous. The population is about seven thousand and the number of houses about one thousand.'

The opening of the Mallow to Killarney railway line in July 1853 gave an extra impetus to the town. Many visitors stayed at the Railway Hotel which opened in July 1854. It was the first railway hotel built in the country. Land for the building was granted to the Great Southern and Western Railway by the Earl of Kenmare without payment, on condition that the train would wait for him. The twenty-one mile extension to Tralee built by the Tralee and Killarney Railway Company was opened in 1859. In 1860, the company was absorbed by the Great Southern and Western Railway. The importance of the area as a tourist amenity was confirmed with the visit of the Prince of Wales, later to become King Edward VII, in 1858 and Queen Victoria in 1861. In 1875 the Kenmare family built an extensive mansion called Kenmare House, in a wooded area, at the edge of the Lower Lake. Fire destroyed the building in 1913.

One of the most impressive houses in Killarney is Muckross House, a Tudor style mansion, built in white Portland stone, which overlooks the middle lake and is close to Muckross Abbey. It was erected for the Herbert family in 1843. At the south-east end of Lough Leane is Muckross Abbey which dates from 1448. It was founded by McCarthy Mór for the Observantine Franciscans and contains the vault of the McCarthy Mórs. At Muckross Lake is a rock where, in Dion Boucicault's play *The Colleen Bawn* and Benedict's opera *The Lily of Killarney*, the heroine was drowned. The story is based on that of a woman who was murdered by drowning off Tarbert and is buried across the Shannon in Clare. The old Muckross cobalt and copper mines opened in 1750 and gave widespread employment locally. A century later the mine was flooded and closed.

In 1916 several members of the local unit of the IRA were arrested and taken to the barracks, which was situated in the Great Southern Hotel. Hours after the killing of Lieutenant O'Connor and four Free State troops in Castleisland on 7 March 1923, five Republican prisoners from Killarney were taken to Countess Bridge and blown up as a reprisal. One escaped.

In 1933 a remarkable feat was achieved in Killarney in the history of Irish film-making. Local garage proprietor, Tom Cooper, produced and directed, with the co-operation of local amateurs, a film called *The Dawn*. Cooper himself headed the excellent cast which also included Eileen Davis, Brian O'Sullivan, Donal O'Cahill and Jerry O'Mahoney. Originally titled *I Am Tainted*, it took from 1933-36 to shoot, as filming was limited to Sunday afternoons and off-peak hours. The consumption of electricity for the indoor scenes equalled the output for the entire Killarney area. There was no basic script and scenes and dialogue were planned only days in advance in local pubs. Few members of the company received wages but some of the 'stars' received payment in the form of drinks and small gifts. The completed film was cut, edited, printed and developed in an old shed behind the cinema. The full-length silent feature film dealt with the IRA and Black and Tan conflict and was very well received.

RECOMMENDED

Muckross House and Gardens.

Muckross Abbey.

Torc Waterfall.

Killarney National Park.

Aghadoe ruins of church and round tower.

St Mary's Cathedral.

Franciscan Friary.

St Mary's Church.

The Poet's Monument, honouring Piaras Ferriter

The National Museum of Irish Transport.

Killarney Races, May and July.

Folk Festival, Easter.

Cultural Centre, traditional music.

Tourist Office in Town Hall.

Ross Castle, (boats for hire).

Golf Course, 18 Holes.

Coach Tours to scenic areas.

Bikes for hire in various shops.

Superbowl Bowling Alley.

Killarney Manor Banquet, Loreto Road, April to October.

Neptune's Killarney Town Hostel.

Scenic Lake Cruises on MV Pride of the Lakes.

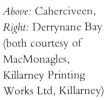

Above: Caherciveen,
Right: Derrynane Bay
(both courtesy of
MacMonagles,
Killarney Printing
Works Ltd, Killarney)

Top left: Mountains and farmland, *Top right:* O'Sullivan's Cascade, *Below:* Kenmare lace,
Previous page: View from Valentia island (all photos by Jan de Fouw), *with inset:* Blennerville Mill
(courtesy of MacMonagles, Killarney Printing Works Ltd, Killarney)

... TRADITIONAL SHOP FRONTS, MAY DAY PILGRIMS ...

Rathmore

The village of Rathmore is east of Killarney and close to Kerry's boundary with County Cork. The name Rathmore means An Ráth Mhór, the Great Rath or Big Ring Fort. Rathmore Castle was one of the many castles throughout Munster to surrender to Sir George Carew in 1600. The Cork-Kerry turnpike (where road tolls were paid) went from Millstreet to Rathmore.

Rathmore has a long main street with shops and houses set well back from the main road. The creamery and community hall dominate the right hand side of the street while on the opposite side there is a monument to the Fifth Battalion, Kerry Number Two Brigade, IRA who were killed in action in the village in 1920. Another feature of the village is the surviving traditional shop fronts and houses with the occupants' names over the front doors.

In 1831 seventy Cistercian monks fled from France and settled in Rathmore. They leased a house and 150 acres for £140 per annum. They had no money for furniture and slept on boxes in the kitchen. Local people went hungry in order to give them alms. The monks also undertook a good deal of renovation on the building. With their rule of silence, when the monks travelled outside the abbey they would lower their heads when approached by local people. The Cistercians remained in Rathmore for five years during which time five of their members died. In 1851 their bodies were exhumed and transferred to Mount Melleray, County Waterford.

Fr Patrick Dinneen, who was born in Rathmore in 1860, compiled an Irish-English dictionary and also edited the poems of O'Donoghue, Ferriter and O'Rahilly.

In 1881 four Presentation Sisters, accompanied by Dr Higgins, the newly-appointed Bishop of Kerry, travelled from Millstreet to Rathmore where they established a convent and school. The nuns were Rev. M. Bernard Barkley, Mother Aloysius Walshe, Sr Bergia Riordan and Sr Agnes Egan.

From the middle of the nineteenth century, people travelled from all over Kerry and Cork to Rathmore on May Day and each succeeding day up to 12 May, which was Old May Day, to 'The City'. The pilgrims wound their way up the steep and winding hillside track to the Penitential station, Craobh Dearg, at the foothills of the Paps Mountains, Dá Chích dAnann, south of the village. They knelt on top and prayed, taking water from the holy well as their forefathers had done for many centuries. The mountains' name means 'the two breasts of Anu'; she was the mother of the mythical Tuatha Dé Danann. The setting is rich in folklore, with legends ranging from a visit by Fionn Mac Cumhail to an ancient residence of Irish kings.

'The City' in the townland of Gortnagown is surrounded by a circular wall ten feet high. Several stones within the enclosure are marked with crosses and circles. A statue of Our Lady of the Wayside was erected at 'The City'. From the twelfth century, this area of Rathmore was a prominent place of pilgrimage and became known as 'the City'.

In 1913 the younger men of the locality formed a company of the Irish Volunteers to demand Home Rule for Ireland. They drilled in the village hall and became the Rathmore E Company, Fifth Battalion, Kerry Number Two Brigade. Some of the men took part in the Easter Rising in Dublin, and others travelled to Fenit in the hope of meeting Roger Casement with his arms shipment.

RECOMMENDED

Monument in Main Street to Old IRA.

Community Hall.

Family names over hall doors.

Craobh Dearg.

Beaufort

The small village of Beaufort is about eight miles from Killarney, off the main road to Killorglin. A signpost to the left leads you over Beaufort Bridge, spanning the River Laune which drains the Lakes of Killarney and carries on to Castlemaine Harbour. The road south from the bridge leads to the Gap of Dunloe. Beaufort (Lios-a-Phúca, Fort of the Fairies) is part of the town land of Coolmagort. Beaufort actually consists of the lands of Beaufort Demesne, lying between the River Laune and the main road. There are two circular earthen fences with a moat or fosse dividing them. It is said to have been the residence of a legendary chieftain of the Tuatha Dé Danann. Ardfergus Hill or Kevin's Leacca is the highest point in the area. Under McCarthy Mór, a local chieftain named Ferris was appointed guardian of the River Laune and had his castle at Ballymalis.

I would recommend a stop at O'Sullivan's pub, which was a centre for film-making over eighty years ago (see below). Further on this road the traveller should stop at a collection of ogham stones. Continuing on you will reach the famed Kate Kearney's Cottage where you can take refreshments. From here jarveys, who do not take too kindly to motorists, will transport visitors by horse and trap or sidecar. Rates can be negotiated. The track up through the Gap of Dunloe is also a favourite route for pony trekking.

In 1795, the eleventh-century O'Mahony Castle of Dunloe near Beaufort was offered for sale and purchased, as a secret gun-powder factory, by the United Irishmen. Napper Tandy was one of those assigned to run it. Being one of the gentry, he mixed with the aristocracy, arousing suspicion amongst the locals. Armed men raided the castle one night and ordered Tandy out. He left, remaining for a time with Parson Day near Dunloe before returning to Dublin. Arthur O'Connor replaced him, and when the United Irishmen no longer required the castle it was repurchased by the O'Mahonys.

In the nineteenth century there were more houses in the village than at present. A narrow road, Green Road, had many craftsmen living there including tailors, smiths, carpenters and wheelwrights. So many tailors lived in the vicinity that the village was once known as 'Tailors' Street'. There were 'Soup Houses' in the village which provided soup for needy Catholic families in famine times during the 1840s and 50s. There was also an attempt at proselytising, as one of the conditions for receiving soup was that the person should attend Protestant services on Christmas Day and one other day.

In 1837, according to Samuel Lewis, there was a constabulary police station and Petty Sessions were heard at Coolmagort every three weeks. The Court House stood at Chapel Cross in Dan O'Shea's field, where offenders received severe sentences for minor crimes. One renowned serious case began at the Court House when Mike Tangney, Gearahmeen, and his cousin Denis Tangney were returned for trial in connection with a shooting in the valley. They were well known moonlighters during the Land League and Land War period. They were tried three times but on each occasion the jury disagreed and they were acquitted. The Petty Sessions continued at Beaufort until 1920 when they were replaced by Sinn Féin Courts.

During the General Election campaign of 1891 Charles Stewart Parnell was forbidden to speak in Killarney. The O'Donoghue, MP for South Kerry, lived

Some films directed by Sidney Olcott and filmed by the Kalem Company in Beaufort.
Above: Kerry Dancers, *right:* Ireland the Oppressed *(1913)*
with Robert Vignola and Mrs Clarke, and below: Rory O'Moore

at Tomies and invited Parnell to speak in his parish. Parnell accepted and held his election meeting in Patrick O'Sullivan's field, south of the Beaufort Hotel. Over a thousand people attended the meeting which was a great success.

At the turn of the century there was a festival in Beaufort on Saint Stephen's Day. Crowds would gather from early morning to engage in set dancing in pubs, on the roads and in the ball alley. They also participated in a game called 'Bataí Buí', a game unique to this area in which teams of four men competed. A stick was stuck in the ground and each player tossed another stick at it and the team with the highest number of strikes won the game. Unfortunately at nightfall, with ample drink consumed, faction fighting easily broke out, often ending in bloodshed.

In 1912 Beaufort Demesne was divided between local farmers. Those who benefited were Ned O'Sullivan, Pat Scully, Jim Coffey, Jack Connor and Michael Galvin.

In 1911 the distinguished American film director, Sidney Olcott, was sent by the Kalem Company to Ireland to make a series of films on Irish themes. Olcott and his company of eight, including Gene Gauntier and Robert Vignola, chose O'Sullivan's Hotel in Beaufort as their headquarters. Many locals were employed as tradesmen and extras in the crowd scenes at a rate of five shillings per day. His first film was *Rory O'Moore* which brought Olcott into confrontation with the clergy over his portrayal of priests and nuns. The American Consul had to resolve the matter with the Bishop of Kerry. In the seventeen weeks they remained in Beaufort they made eighteen short films about the trials of the rebels. The company, which became affectionately known as the O'Kalems, returned to Beaufort in 1912, 1913 and 1914, producing such films as *Ireland the Oppressed*, *The Colleen Bawn*, *Arrah-na-Pogue* and *Kerry Dancers*. The films were released in America and Europe and were well received. With the outbreak of World War One in 1914 the company returned to America, never to return, so ending their activities and plans to build a studio.

When Volunteers from all over Kerry assembled in Killarney for a show of strength, intrigue surrounded the appearance of the squad from Beaufort. While all other squads paraded with dummy guns the Beaufort men carried authentic rifles and everybody was mystified as to how they acquired them. On making enquiries the officer commanding was informed that they were film props from the Kalem Company, kindly loaned by Sidney Olcott, who enjoyed the humour of the situation.

Almost all the young men in the parish joined the Volunteers and there was an active group locally, totalling over one hundred. The captain commanding was Ned O'Sullivan of Beaufort. The headquarters of the Kerry Number Two Brigade was in O'Connor's house in the Gap of Dunloe. Sinn Féin Courts were established in the parish in 1918. They held regular sittings in secret, to which people came with their complaints, and English Courts were boycotted. Jerry Doyle of Whitefield was the Supreme Judge and Paddy Leane of Tullig was Chief Constable. The Brigade launched many attacks against the British Army and Black and Tans and when the RIC evacuated the barracks in 1919 they burned it down. (A garda barracks was built in 1932). In the Civil War most of the Beaufort Volunteers took the Republican side. When a company of Free State troops took over Beaufort House local men retreated into the mountains and lived rough in dug-outs.

RECOMMENDED

Kate Kearney's Cottage.
Gap of Dunloe.
Ogham Stones.
O'Sullivan's Pub, Beaufort.
Churchtown, Family Farm
Park, May - September.

Castleisland

Castleisland, a market town, is situated at the eastern boundary of the county where the Limerick Road crosses the Ahanowen River. In Irish the parish was called Oileán Chiarraí, the Island of Kerry, as north of the River Maine was once known as Kerry and south of the river as Desmond. In 1200 King John granted the northern section of the county to the Norman knight, Meiler FitzHenry, but the land reverted to the Crown when he entered a monastery. The town evolved its name from a castle built there in 1226 by his successor, the English Justiciar, Geoffrey de Marisco. This was the renowned Castell of the Island — created artificially by turning the waters of the Maine into a moat around the castle. De Marisco built a number of castles in defensive positions along the River Maine. His daughter, Eleanor, inherited the castle and it came into the control of the Geraldines.

Whenever I visit the town of Castleisland I am struck by its long, wide main street which is an open invitation not alone to double but to treble park. Tractors, vans, cars and motorbikes are abandoned rather than parked as their owners go about their business. Another strong feature of the town is the number of surviving traditional shop fronts: among the most picturesque are W. O'Connor's, Wren's and O'Hussey's. Also of interest is the gothic style Catholic Church, a left turn off the main street. A short distance outside the town is Crag Cave which is open to visitors.

During the rule of the first Earl of Desmond in 1345 the new Viceroy, Sir Raoul D'Ufford, summoned a parliament in Dublin on 7 June but the Earl refused to attend and instead called another assembly in Callan, County Kilkenny. D'Ufford marched with a strong force to Castleisland, the Earl's stronghold. The Earl's knights, Eustace Le Poer and William Le Grant, refused to obey the Viceroy and offered resistance. After a two-week siege the castle was taken. The knights, along with the Earl's seneschal, John Cotterel, were hanged, drawn and quartered in front of the castle. The Earl and his wife evaded capture. Queen Elizabeth I granted the castle, town and adjoining lands of 12,000 acres to Sir William Herbert and his family in March 1589. During the revolt of 1598 the Herberts abandoned their Castleisland estate for a period. In 1600 Irish forces captured and burned the castle, but soon after Thomas Herbert had it rebuilt.

In *A Tour in Ireland* in 1779 Arthur Young wrote: 'About Castleisland the land is very good, ranking among the best in Kerry. From that place to Arbella House, the land is as good as the management bad, every field over-run with all kinds of rubbish, the fences in ruins, and no appearance but of desolation: they were mowing some fine crops of hay, which I suppose will be made in the snow.'

There was little activity in Kerry during the 1798 Rising but the Charter School in Castleisland, which was occupied by local yeomanry, was attacked by the rebels and three of the garrison were killed. Following the famine of 1821 the Government promoted the building of roads. Limestone quarries went into operation and shell, gravel and coral sand were also used. A forty-two mile stretch was opened, linking Castleisland and Killarney to Mallow. The town was noted for its red marble quarry, stone from which was used in the building of Honan Chapel, adjoining University College, Cork.

During the Great Famine of the mid-1840s cabbage was extensively used as a substitute food in the district. One particularly bad month in the town was referred to as 'July of the Cabbage'. Nettles were also eagerly sought by hungry people who boiled them as food.

The Gothic style church was designed by George Ashlin and Augustus Welby Pugin. The Presentation Sisters ran a convent in Castleisland from which they intended to extend the order to other locations in the county. Three of the sisters were sent to establish a convent in Kenmare in 1859 but they ran into difficulties with the parish priest and within two years had to abandon their plans and return to Castleisland. In 1878 the sisters opened another convent in Sneem but it did not succeed either and they also had to return to the mother house.

During a by-election in February 1872 one of the candidates, a Catholic liberal, J.A. Dease, was attacked and injured in the town. An important incentive to the commercial life of the town was the opening on 30 August 1875 of a ninety-five mile railway branch line from Gortatlea to Castleisland by the Castleisland Railway Company. It was the first light railway system in the country.

On 30 March 1882 the notorious murder of Arthur Herbert, an unpopular magistrate, occurred just outside the town. His family had been in Castleisland since 1580 when they were granted land under the plantation of Munster. Herbert was a judge of the Petty Sessions and was a despised figure because of evictions and the handing down of stiff sentences. On the day of the murder he sentenced John Casey, a farm labourer, to one month in jail for being drunk and disorderly. That night while walking home Herbert was shot dead by assassins who lay in wait at Lisheen Bawn Cross. The Government offered a £2,000 reward for the conviction of his murderers. John Casey and James Brown were arrested but never convicted as no witnesses came forward. A popular ballad was written about the incident by Johnny Patterson.

A special police tax, previously imposed upon the inhabitants of the district, was abolished in 1884. The town was a centre of considerable bitterness and unrest from the Land War to the Civil War period. A large meeting in support of the Irish Volunteers was held in the town in April 1914 and a local branch of the Volunteers was subsequently formed. In May 1916 the London Scottish regiment moved into Castleisland and arrested a number of men, including Daniel O'Mahony, commander of the Volunteers who was later jailed in Wakefield Jail. Many ambushes and attacks were planned on the British forces in the area but most were not brought to fruition. On 6 March 1923 Lieutenant O'Connor, noted for his cruel methods while interrogating Republican prisoners, was killed by a mine along with two other officers and two Free State troopers at Knocknagoshel. Many reprisals occurred throughout the county as a result of the atrocity.

Due to coal shortages following the Second World War, ten branch lines of the railway, including the one to Castleisland, were closed to traffic from 27 January 1947.

A recent addition to the tourist amenities of the area is Crag Cave, an ancient fossil cave system. Local folklore associates Crag Cave with Diarmuid and Gráinne, who are believed to have spent a night there during their flight from Fionn Mac Cumhail. The Geological Survey of 1859 mentioned that 'In the townland of Crag, north-west of Castleisland, there are caves worn by water, some of which may be transversed for some distance'. The existence of the cave was known for many decades but it was only in 1983 that Martyn Farr, a Welsh cave diver, discovered the opening. The many stalactites and stalagmites which grace the cave have taken many thousands of years to form. The special lighting and atmospheric music do much to enhance the cave. It was opened to the public in the summer of 1989 and was officially opened by Charles Haughey in May 1991.

DESMOND CASTLE (remains)
CASTLEISLAND

RECOMMENDED

Crag Cave.
Traditional shop fronts.
Memory Lane Museum.
Old pump at end of Main Street.
Catholic Church.
Shoemaker's Inn, traditional music.

... WHERE HORSES ARE CHANGED ...

Farranfore

The small village of Farranfore, An Fearann Fuar (the Cold Land), is situated at a junction between the Slieve Mish Mountains and close to Castleisland. The Farranfore River, An Feit Fionn (the Fair Stream), flows through the village.

Farranfore could be termed the crossroads of County Kerry from which the traveller can take diverse routes. This is a good place to stop and study the signposts and guidebooks before proceeding. Nowhere in Kerry will a weary traveller be far from a drink and Farranfore is no exception; despite its size it has several fine pubs. The old railway station and the airport are also worth a visit. On Sunday afternoon visitors can take flights and, for the more adventurous, flying lessons are available.

In 1830 Farranfore was chosen as a neutral venue for a famous cock fight. The competitors were 'Mulroon', a champion cock from Killarney, and 'The Dancing Master' from Castleisland. Hundreds of supporters from each town arrived to cheer on their own cock. Following a few preliminary bouts the main event began. 'The Dancing Master' made one lunge and his spur sank into 'Mulroon's' head and the champion of a hundred fights lay dead. Then followed a vicious bare-knuckle fight between the opposing factions.

William Makepeace Thackeray in *The Irish Sketch Book* of 1842 was very scathing in his assessment of Farranfore. 'You pass through a sad-looking, bare, undulating country, with few trees, and poor stone hedges, and poorer crops; nor have I yet taken in Ireland so dull a ride. About half way between Tralee and Killarney is a wretched town, where horses are changed, and where I saw more hideous begging than anywhere else, I think. And I was glad to get over this gloomy tract of country, and enter the capital of Kerry.'

The local boys' national school was erected in the townland of Knockadirah in 1841. The girls' school opened the following year. Teachers in each school received a salary of eight pounds per annum.

On the Ordnance Survey Map of 1845 the Turnpike (toll road) and Toll Gate are clearly visible. The village was then also known as 'The Pike' because of this feature. Up to the 1850s a Bianconi stage coach en route from Cork to Tralee stopped to change horses at Farranfore for the second part of the journey. This service ceased with the arrival of the railway in 1856. The station master's wife ran a tearoom, adjoining the station. Plans to build a branch line from Farranfore to Killarney were approved in 1871 but the contractors for the railway found great difficulty in hiring labourers in Milltown, Castlemaine and Killorglin due to high emigration. Work did not commence for a decade and the twelve-mile track finally opened on 15 January 1885. Eight years later the line was extended to Cahirciveen and Valentia Island. It ceased operation in 1960.

The police barracks in the village was built by Lord Kenmare in 1873 and was staffed by six constables and a sergeant. The Black and Tans occupied the barracks between 1918 and 1921. In November 1920 two Black and Tans were shot dead by the IRA in the station. The following day several Crossley Tenders of Black and Tans burned Ulick O'Sullivan's pub and other buildings in reprisal. During the Civil War the barracks was held by the Republicans when Free State troops invaded the village. The 'Staters' opened fire and the Republicans were forced to evacuate the building which was badly damaged during the exchange.

Bishop Eamonn Casey (former Bishop of Kerry, who resigned as Bishop of Galway in 1992 following the 'Annie Murphy' affair) was born in Fieries, close to Farranfore, in 1927. In the late 1960s an enthusiastic group formed a committee with the intention of planning and building 'the fourth largest airport in Ireland' in Kerry. Sixty acres of land were acquired from farmers in the Farranfore area and a company was formed. The Government provided a grant of fifty per cent of the £60,000 cost and the company raised the balance through a share issue. The first flight landed at Farranfore Airport on 13 August 1969. Over the years there was a steady growth in facilities and July 1979 saw the inauguration of the first scheduled air service from Farranfore to Dublin. During the Farranfore Air Show of 1984, Concorde made a flyover.

Today, services operate from Farranfore to Dublin, Manchester and London. The airport has taken steps to market the tourist potential of the area including golfing, fishing, sea sports and equestrian activities.

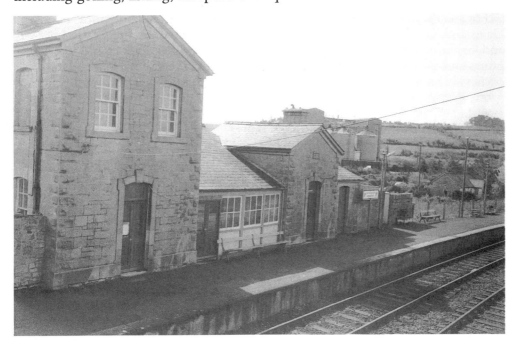

Left: Farranfore railway station, and below: Kerry County Airport, Farrafore

RECOMMENDED

Old railway station. Farranfore Airport. Trips available on Sunday afternoons. Flying lessons are also available.

Castlemaine

There was a wild colonial boy,
Jack Duggan was his name,
He was born and reared in Ireland
In a place called Castlemaine.
He was his father's only son,
His mother's pride and joy,
And dearly did his parents love the wild colonial boy.

The village of Castlemaine, Caisleán na Mainge (the Castle of Maine) is situated at the southern end of the Dingle peninsula on the River Maine. The name is derived from the small river, the Maine, which runs through the village. North of the village begin the Slieve Mish range of mountains.

For such a small village Castlemaine can still boast of four fine pubs. James Day's and Knightly's Bar face each other. The other two are the Castle Inn and Griffin's. Two other places worth noting in the village are an old water pump and the Old Colonial Boy Art Gallery and Coffee Shop. The genial owner will liberally dispense information on accommodation and local beauty spots. Within the vicinity farmhouse and country house accommodation is available. West of Castlemaine is the village of Bolteens where traditional music sessions can be enjoyed in many pubs.

According to the Annals of Innisfallen, in 1215 the Geraldine invaders, Maurice and John Fitzgerald, built Castell Magne, a fortress of importance. The castle was on a rock in the middle of the river to protect their newly conquered territory from the McCarthys and played an important part in the Elizabethan wars. It had a high tower with a flat roof and battlements. The river was a dividing line between the territories of the Desmonds and the McCarthys. Two rebels named Moriarty and Kelly killed the Earl of Desmond in Glounaneenta and brought his head to claim their bounty. Queen Elizabeth paid her subjects. Kelly was later hanged at Tyburn for robbery.

Thomas Spring, Warden of Castle Maine, was granted possession of Killagha Abbey and its lands. It remained a Desmond Castle until the revolt of James Fitzmaurice. In 1571 during the first Desmond War the English under Perrott regarded Castlemaine as being of prime importance due to its strategic location and made an unsuccessful bid to capture it. On Christmas Eve 1572, the Prior of Killagha Abbey with thirty of his brethren entered Castlemaine Castle to celebrate Mass. The following day, the Earl of Desmond began a three-month siege after which he took the castle, enabling him to cross the river at will.

Over the next eighty years the castle and Desmond lands became the main objective of the Queen and her army. It was the centre of several attacks and sieges and in turn became the stronghold of the Desmonds and the McCarthys. In 1652 Cromwellian troops under Colonel Ludlow attacked and captured it. Queen Elizabeth I appointed a constable to the castle, a post which continued up to 1832.

The poor of the locality lived in deplorable conditions in primitive cabins. In 1839 the Commissioners for Woods built a quay at Castlemaine from which many of the peasant families emigrated to America following the 1840s famine.

For a time a lucrative import/export trade existed at Castlemaine but it lost much of this trade through the silting of the river and the deposition of a considerable sandbar at its mouth. A four arch bridge was constructed over the river and the adjacent mudflats made a suitable sanctuary for bird life.

Castlemaine was the birthplace of Jack Donoghue, who left his native place at the end of the nineteenth century and went to live in Australia where he changed his name to Jack Duggan. He became a bush ranger and gained quite a reputation 'by robbing the rich to feed the poor'. He was killed by mounted police and is commemorated in song as the 'Wild Colonial Boy'.

On 8 March 1923 some Republican prisoners escaped while clearing mines at Castlemaine.

Close to Castlemaine, at Ardcanaght, stands a huge boulder, weighing four tons. It is one of the most important ancient inscribed stones in the county.

OVERLOOKING CASTLEMAINE HARBOUR

RECOMMENDED

Bird watching at Castlemaine Harbour.

West of the village at Ardcanaght is an old burial ground with two ogham stones and a huge standing stone.

The Old Colonial Boy Art Gallery and Coffee Shop, also for tourist information.

Old water pump.

... TO KILLAGHA AND KILCOLEMAN ABBEYS ...

Milltown

The village of Milltown, Baile an Mhuilinn (Town of the Mill), is situated on the road from Castlemaine to Killorglin. The parish of Milltown in earlier times was referred to as the Parish of Kilcoleman. There were eighteen townlands in the parish and many of them were densely wooded. The earliest inhabitants of the parish were the O'Connells, ancestors of the Liberator, Daniel O'Connell, who remained in possession until the Norman invasion. In 1169 an Anglo-Norman force under Justiciar Geoffrey de Marisco, Strongbow's nephew, moved west along the Maine River and took over the parish lands of Kilcoleman beside the river. The Fitzgeralds, a Norman family, built a castle at Callinaferry. The road from Milltown to Killarney, dating from 1300, was one of the oldest roads in the county and the one on which most invaders passed.

At first glance Milltown would appear to be little more than an attractive village but it is rich in history. For anyone seeking information on the locality a call to Stephen Cotter in his pub 'The Plough' is a must. He is an authority on all aspects of the history and folklore of the area. Local people have been very active in fund-raising for the restoration of Killagha Abbey. To reach the Abbey take the Killorglin road and after a mile and a half follow the signpost pointing right to the Abbey. I would also recommend a visit to the ruins of the big house, Kilcoleman Abbey. Beside the gates of the Abbey there is a helpful map indicating places of interest. The colourful Presentation Convent stands in welcome contrast to many of the sombre looking schools throughout the country. Early morning visitors are rewarded by the aroma of freshly baked bread from Larkin's Bakery. The village is twinned with St Nicolas du Pelem in France.

Geoffrey de Marisco founded Killagha Priory (Cill-Achaidh, the Church of the Field) for the Canons Regulars of St Augustine in 1215. He directed that only Englishmen could become members of the order and the rule was rigidly enforced for two centuries. The Prior was a Lord of Parliament, but owing to the distance between London and his place of residence, he was seldom summoned. Killagha was to become the richest of the Augustinian priories in Ireland with the monks paying a £50 tax per year. The Priory was also known as the Abbey of Our Lady Mary de Bello Loco. A leper house was built close to the priory.

With the constant change of ownership and the claiming of land after battles the McCarthys took over sizeable tracts of land in Kilcoleman. There followed a long running feud between the English and natives. Killagha Priory was suppressed in 1576 and along with large tracts of land was granted to Captain Thomas Spring. The property was fortified by the Spring family during the Cromwellian war and was later granted to Major John Godfrey, a Cromwellian officer. He also received the confiscated land of the McCarthys and in total got around five thousand acres.

From 1649-53 the Springs, McCarthys, McCrohans and many priests who went into hiding worshipped at the Mass Rock in Killacloghane Wood. Fr Boethius Eagan, Fr Thaddeus Moriarty, prior of the Dominican House in Tralee, and another man were arrested in the wood by Cromwellian soldiers and taken to Killarney where they were executed on 15 October 1653. The families of the Springs, McCarthys and McCrohans were later expelled to West Clare. The English built the first Protestant church in the parish, the ruins of which are now known as 'The White Church'. Under the Penal Laws the first Catholic church in the village had to be built a hundred feet back from the street. Near Milltown is Poulnaraha (the Hole of the Rath or Fort), an enclosed area, 135 feet in diameter. Another important site is Fort Agnes, a ringed fort.

With the Act of Settlement the Godfreys were committed to settling English families in the village. The planters built their village and introduced crafts and trades including a tannery and linen industry. As a result in the early 1700s the village became known as Milltown. The manufacture of linen continued until the 1800s. In 1773 Sir John Godfrey, first Baronet of the line, built a mansion at Kilcoleman and a water-powered mill which operated for over a century. In 1819 he added an additional wing, the same year the Church of Ireland church was erected. The church with a square tower was completed in 1822. The following year Sir John Godfrey gave land to the Catholic community to build a new church and later made a similar gift to the Methodists. A new impetus was added to Milltown when a Dutch engineer was commissioned to bank the tidal waters of the River Maine, transforming it into a small port capable of berthing a large variety of vessels. By the early nineteenth century, local families had formed a thriving new community. Around that period a trading vessel arrived at the old quay near the abbey and stole one of the mullions and part of the tracery of the east window of Killagha Priory.

In 1920 local members of the RIC were ordered to hand over the barracks to British troops and to transfer to outlying stations. Several refused, and resigned in protest.

RECOMMENDED

Killagha Abbey.
Mass Rock.
White Church.
Killacloghane Wood, ideal for walking.
Heritage Centre.
Mart for Cattle and Sheep.
The Plough pub (for local history).

Dingle Peninsula

On leaving Tralee and crossing the bridge at Blennerville you enter the Dingle Peninsula (Corca Dhuibhne). Continue on this road for about ten miles until you meet a fork in the road where you will have to make a decision. The signposts inform you that Dingle is in both directions! The left-hand road, a leisurely route through the villages of Camp, Lispole and Annascaul, is

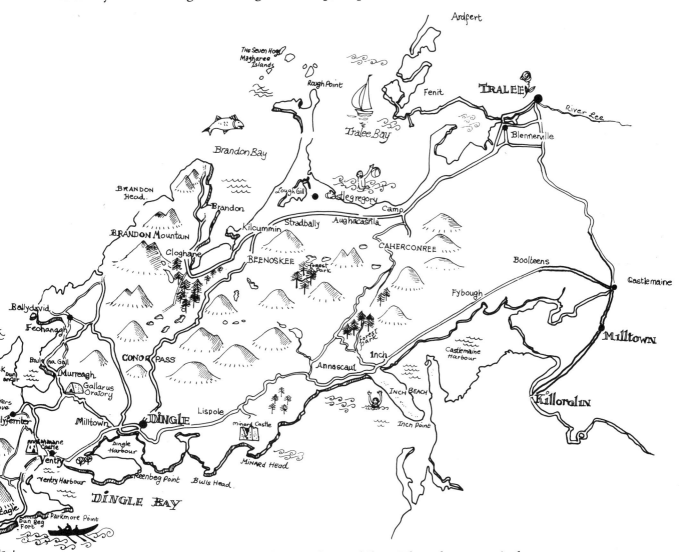

recommended for laden cars, trucks, coaches or bikes. The other route is the more scenic but hazardous Conor Pass where frequent mists can reduce visibility to ten feet. This route is not advisable for inexperienced drivers, caravans or uninitiated cyclists. We will proceed by way of this route and return by the former. Having negotiated the 1,500-foot-high Conor Pass, the traveller can enjoy a panoramic view of Dingle Bay and the many dark lakes. The good news is that the remainder of the journey is four miles downhill to Dingle.

Castlegregory

Castlegregory is a small coastal village on the northern side of the Dingle peninsula. There are several interpretations of the name Castlegregory. One version indicated that it was named after Pope Gregory the Great, who claimed to be of Irish origin. The more obvious explanation is that it developed from Gregory Hoare who built a castle there early in the sixteenth century (Caisleán Ghriaire, Gregory's Castle). His stronghold stood at the south-east of the village, later known as Castle Lane.

Leave the main Tralee to Dingle road at Stradbally where you will find an ogham stone. Proceeding northwards you will reach the small village of Castlegregory. The area is most noted for its long golden beach and sand-dunes. It is ideal for swimming, sailboarding and fishing. Castlegregory Furniture is a remarkable furniture factory in the village which offers a range of outstanding furniture at low prices.

The village is situated at the neck of a spit and is the gateway to the Maharees, a narrow strip of dunes, and a sandy beach which divides Tralee Bay on the east from Brandon Bay on the west. The lagoon lake of Lough Gill was formed through the accumulation of shingle. In the vicinity there are the remains of an early Christian burial ground. From above Scraggane pier the Seven Hogs, a group of islands, can be clearly seen. On one of the islands there are monastic huts and clochauns. Close to Castlegregory is a gallaun (standing stone) over twelve feet high. North of Scraggane Bay are the remains of Kilshannig church which has an early cross-pillar.

At the beginning of the sixteenth century Gregory Hoare lived in conflict with his neighbour William Moore, another Desmond tenant, and a dispute over their boundary became so serious that the case came before the Desmond seneschal court in Dingle. The court found against Hoare and he became so outraged that he became paralysed. This predicament gave Hoare's son, Black Hugh, the opportunity to marry Moore's daughter, Ellen. It was hoped that the union would bring about a temporary easing of the feud but as the bridal party made its way through Castlegregory, Gregory Hoare attempted to block their path. Moore pushed him aside and Hoare died on the spot.

In 1580 Lord Deputy Grey, en route to attack Fort-del-Ore (now Dún an Óir, the Fort of Gold), requested Black Hugh Hoare to hold his castle against the Irish. Hoare, a loyal subject of the Queen, prepared a banquet for his guests. Grey went directly to Smerwick Harbour but Edmund Spenser, Sir Walter Raleigh and other officers stopped at Castlegregory. Ellen, loyal to the Irish cause, resented this intrusion of their privacy and deliberately emptied all the wine kegs. Black Hugh became so angry at her action that he stabbed her to death. Black Hugh was arrested and taken to Gallarus Castle for trial but died suddenly close to where his father had died.

The only daughter of the union married Walter Hussey of Castlegregory and Dingle. Hussey, a supporter of the Knight of Kerry, was granted the castle but when it was attacked by Cromwellian forces he was forced to escape. He sought refuge in Minard Castle but when Minard was later attacked Hussey and his men were killed. Following the war the remaining members of the Hussey family were reduced to poverty. Thereafter Castlegregory was granted to a Cromwellian officer, Captain Anthony Shortcliffe. In 1800 the first Lord

Ventry, Thomas Mullin of Dingle, took possession of the village and it remained in the Ventry family until 1913.

By the beginning of the 1800s there were approximately a thousand inhabitants living in the village, mainly in thatched cottages. The Catholic church was built in 1831. Close to the village is the Washing Bridge, so called because the women gathered there to do their washing every Monday. From the 1800s the Clais Garbh races were held on the beach there every September until they were transferred to Loughbeg.

South of the village is St Brendan's Church of Ireland church. Nearby are the remains of a fifteenth-century church in which the family vault of the Fitzgerald family is situated. There are two ancient stone crosses in the graveyard, one dating to the seventh century and the other to the ninth. There is a headstone to the crew members of the barque *Fort Yarrock* of Glasgow who lost their lives in Brandon Bay when they were shipwrecked on 29 January 1894, following a voyage from California. Seven of the crew were buried in Castlegregory and Brandon and five at Stradbally.

Like so many other villages Castlegregory also enjoyed a 'Pattern Day' on 15th August each year. In earlier times only the men attended Pattern Day and the women gathered the following day which was known as 'Sheilas's Day'. By the turn of the century many trades were flourishing in the village including carpenters, shoemakers, coopers, blacksmiths, bakers, butchers and tailors.

In 1891 a six-mile branch line of the Tralee-Dingle Railway was extended to Castlegregory. The narrow gauge line was built by the Tralee and Dingle Railway Company. There was an element of risk on this route and passengers were advised to travel by rail to Castlegregory and then by other means over the Conor Pass to Dingle. On Whit Monday 1893 a train carrying passengers and pigs ran down a bank close to Castlegregory Junction. The engine and some carriages fell thirty feet, killing three people and ninety pigs. On 17 April 1939 the branch line was declared uneconomic and was closed to all traffic. The sleepers were sold for a penny each.

Cross at St Brendan's church, Castlegregory

RECOMMENDED

Ogham stone.

Lough Gill, Scraggane Bay and Kilshannig Point for fishing.

Castlegregory Furniture.

Brandon Bay Caravan Park.

The Warren Caravan Park.

Spillane's Bar for seafood.

Castlegregory Golf and Fishing Club, 9 Hole Golf Course.

The Crutches Hotel and Cottages.

Cloghane

Descending the Conor Pass from the Dingle side, take the first turn left to the picturesque village of Cloghane. The village faces a wide expanse of beach, sea and mountains. Neatly cared for, with a colourful array of window boxes, Cloghane has some pleasant pubs and is a good base for exploring on foot. This is the easiest side to approach a climb of Mount Brandon.

Cloghane is a coastal village on the northern side of the Dingle peninsula beneath Mount Brandon and the Conor Pass where the Owenmore River flows into Cloghane Creek. The name Cloghane in Irish is An Clochán (the Stone House or perhaps the Stepping Stones). The village has existed since the thirteenth century but there is scant information as to its early history.

In the early 1800s the village consisted of forty-three small thatched dwellings and a flour mill. The old Catholic church was built in 1824 and the present sandstone church called St Brendan's was built at the beginning of this century. The Protestant church was built in 1828 when there was a Church of Ireland revival in Kerry. In the church there is a stone carving of the head of Crom Dubh (the Dark One), a mythological chieftain. A pilgrimage was regularly held to the summit of Mount Brandon up to the early part of this century to commemorate the conversion to Christianity of Crom Dubh. The ritual was an extension of the celebrations to the God Lugh. The road led to the summit from the small mountain hamlet of Faha (Faithche, a Green Level Field) on the Cloghane side; and from Kilmalcheadar they followed the pathway. They took the easy route to the summit and the more hazardous track on the return journey.

In 1837 Samuel Lewis recorded: 'The village, near the shore of the bay, contains thirty-five dwellings, all thatched; and in it are situated the parochial church, a Roman Catholic chapel and school.'

A small pier was erected by the Fishery Board to facilitate the men who fished in yawls and canoes. During the season up to 150 men were engaged in fishing and they spent the remainder of the year farming. On several occasions over the years, schools of porpoises became stranded at low tide on the beach at Cloghane. The first recorded date was in June 1854, a period of hunger and depression, when the locals cut up the carcasses for food. Other schools were washed up and on Pattern Day in 1918 a school of porpoises was stranded. In November 1965 sixty-three pilot whales, each measuring up to twenty feet, were stranded on the beach.

The RIC barracks was evacuated and burned during the campaign of 1920. On Tuesday 20 August 1940 a World War Two German Luftwaffe Condor bomber was forced to crashland in a mist on Faha Mountain. The six-man crew, under Lieutenant Kurt Mollenhauer, made their way down the mountain to Cloghane, where they were warmly greeted by the locals. They were taken to the local garda barracks and later interned in the Curragh Military Camp. The aluminium cross on Brandon's summit was made of spars from the crashed plane. In recent years Kurt Mollenhauer has made a nostalgic return visit to the village.

Several British planes also crashed in the Cloghane area in 1943. On 28 July, a BOAC Sunderland crashed, ten of the twenty-five on board being killed. On 22 August eight of the eleven men on board an RAF Sunderland were killed.

All six of the Polish crew of an RAF Wellington were killed on 20 December. The community in Cloghane have erected a plaque to the memory of all those who lost their lives.

In 1983 Cloghane was chosen by Argentine director, Martin Donovan, as the location for a feature film, *Sense of Wonder*. Of the 150 local people employed on the film, twenty-eight had speaking parts and three of the Kerry brogues had to be dubbed for the international market. The film starred Anne Chaplin, the youngest daughter of Charlie, in her film debut. During the three weeks of shooting, the sixty strong crew took up every available bed in the village. Donovan's screenplay was based on the death of his seventeen-year-old brother in a car crash. He changed the script on numerous occasions to move the action outdoors to avail of the magnificent scenery. The film had its first public showing in Dingle's Phoenix Cinema in 1984.

Left: Headstone to the crew of the Fort Yarrock of Glasgow, lost in Brandon Bay in 1894. Right: Cloghane old Protestant church

RECOMMENDED

Old Protestant church.

St Brendan's Catholic Church.

Plaque to pilots killed in Second World War.

Aluminium cross on Mount Brandon.

O'Connor's Pub.

Ó Súilleabháin's Pub.

... FRESH FISH, MOUNTAIN TOPS, REGATTAS ...

Brandon

The small village of Brandon is on the northern side of the Dingle peninsula, a little beyond Cloghane. About 1200 the tribe of Uí Fearba were active on the northern side of the pensinula around Brandon. The village is noted for its sandy beaches, extending along Brandon Bay. Towering above the coastal village is Mount Brandon (Cnoc Bhréanainn, St Brendan's Hill), the second highest mountain in the country, rising 3,127 feet above sea-level. Below the summit are St Brendan's Well, the remains of St Brendan's Oratory and the ruins of several penitential stations.

Well worth a visit is Nora Murphy's pub above the harbour where on a fine day customers can enjoy their drinks outdoors as they watch the activity on the pier. Fresh fish can be bought directly from fishermen. Don't miss the nearby Brandon Point and Brandon Head. On a clear day, climb the head where the view will well compensate for the effort. A look-out post was erected on Brandon Point during World War Two.

The first pier at Brandon was built in 1825 to facilitate over two hundred fishermen who engaged in herring fishing in the vicinity. Later a coast-guard station was erected above the pier. A new pier was erected in 1889 when there was extensive mackerel fishing which lasted until 1914. There was a spin-off industry with women and children gutting, salting and packing mackerel into barrels for export to America. Some of the barrels were transported to Castlegregory for export to England.

The townland of Murirrigane, north of the pier, was once the home of the Geraldine sept, Sliocht Edmund, whose family held control of the area around Brandon Bay. With the defeat of the Earl of Desmond and his Geraldine followers in 1583 Sliocht Edmund lost the estate.

Brandon Point (Srón Bhrain, Bran's Nose), a mile and a half north of the village, is said to be where the mythical traveller Bran and his followers landed after a voyage to the Other World. Not realising that they had been away for hundreds of years one of the group, Nechtan, jumped on to land and immediately crumbled into dust. On witnessing the fate of his colleague, Bran upped anchor and was never seen or heard of again. Some sources indicate that Brandon took its name from Bran. About the middle of the sixth century St Brendan founded a monastery here and the settlement was to give his name to the mountain. For many centuries the mountain became a place of pilgrimage. It is reputed that Brendan had prayed for several days on the summit of Mount Brandon when an angel appeared and conveyed to him details of the voyage which would earn him the title 'Brendan the Navigator'. He was then about sixty and was absent from Ireland for about seven years.

The ancient burial ground of Currauly has an early cross–pillar. On Pattern Day the pilgrims followed the Saint's Road from Ballybrack village to the summit of Brandon Mountain, marked by the Stations of the Cross.

In 1978 Brandon was the location for a feature film *Cry of the Innocent* with Rod Taylor and Cyril Cusack. The popular Brandon regatta was revived in recent years and has again become a great spectacle for competitors and locals alike.

House near Kilmalkedar where monks lived in former times, now known locally as Brendan's house.

RECOMMENDED

Brandon pier.

Brandon Point.

Brandon Regatta, July.

Brandon Arts Gallery and Studio of Michael Flaherty.

O'Shea's Pub for salmon and chips.

Weaver's Art Gallery.

Brandon Sea Angling Centre.

Benagh Restaurant.

Nora Murphy's Pub.

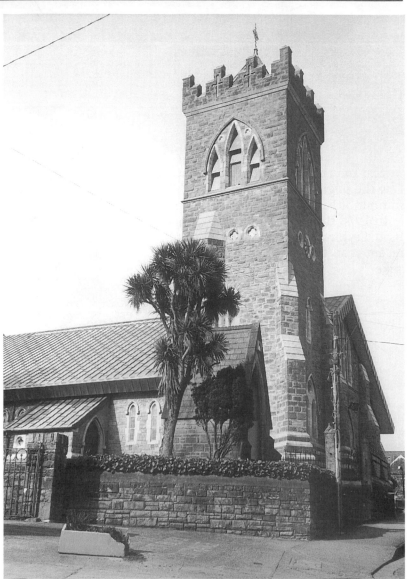

Above: Dingle harbour
Right: Dingle Catholic church

... RESTAURANTS, RACES, REGATTAS AND A DOLPHIN ...

Dingle

Dingle, a small hilly town, is one of the main fishing ports on the west coast and the chief town on the Dingle peninsula. It was once a fortress, surrounded by a wall, hence its name in Irish 'An Daingean' — the fortress or, according to Richard Hayward in *In the Kingdom of Kerry*, the fortress of O'Cush (they were chieftains here before the English invaded). The Annals of the Four Masters call it 'Daingean Uí Chúis' (the fort of O'Chush).

During the summer months Dingle becomes a cosmopolitan town with thousands of Europeans enjoying the scenery, food and crack. Fungie the dolphin has become the town's biggest attraction with television crews and tourists from all over Europe travelling to see his antics. The best viewing place to see him is on the path leading from the Skelligs Hotel to the lighthouse. For a closer look you can travel out by fishing boat from the pier. Dingle caters for all tastes, from the backpackers in hostels, to the family hotels like the Skelligs, the Hillgrove and Benners, from rented cottages to tranquil B&Bs. The town is also a good base for walking and cycling with many shops renting out bikes. Browsers will be well rewarded with antique shops, craft and pottery shops and the highly regarded bookshop, An Café Liteartha. The prolific firm of Brandon Book Publishers is based in the town. On the coast road the Ceardlann Craft Village is worth a visit to see native crafts in production. At the top of Main Street is a large bullaun which fascinates tourists. The Tourist Office in Main Street is only open during the summer season. For its size the town must contain the largest number of high class restaurants in the country. In recent years a number of medium priced restaurants have been opened. From personal experience I would recommend several: the Half Door, Doyle's, Máire de Barra's pub and restaurant for bacon and cabbage, Cúl an Tí, a health food restaurant and Sméara Dubha, a vegetarian restaurant. There is no shortage of venues for music and a visit will not be complete without dropping into O'Flaherty's and An Droichead Beag.

The remoteness of the town did not deter Anglo-Norman or English invaders from attacking it. An Anglo-Norman family named Hussey, after whom the town was also reputed to have been named, were granted lands there in the thirteenth century by the Desmonds. The Knights of Kerry, a branch of the Desmonds, were the town's most prominent family. There is a Desmond tomb dated 1504 in the Protestant churchyard.

Hooker's *Chronicle* of 1850 gives the following report; 'The Erle of Ormond, who nener slept his time but was alwaies in readiness, divideth his companie into three partes and so marched to Dingle-a-Cush; and as they went they drove the whole countrie before them into Ventrie and by that means they preid and tooke alle the cattell in the countrie to the number of eighte thousand kine besides horses, garrons, shepe and gotes; and alle such people as they met they did without mercie putte to the sword.'

The Husseys built a castle and developed an enterprising business of exporting hides and wool. It built up a flourishing trade with Spain from the fourteenth century. Many Spaniards settled in Dingle and there was inter-marrying between traders and natives. St James' Church of Ireland church was named after the patron saint of Spain and was said to have been built by Spaniards in 1804.

The emissary of King Charles of Spain was received in 1529 by James, eleventh Earl of Desmond. In 1585 Dingle became the only chartered borough in Kerry and Queen Elizabeth contributed £300 towards erecting a wall around the new borough. At one period the town had three castles. State papers of 1576 describe it as a stronghold or walled town with a large tower at either end. The third castle was part of the fortification. Many British soldiers settled in the town after the Smerwick massacre in 1580. A later charter was confirmed by James I and the town became incorporated, permitting it to elect a mayor called a Sovereign, with symbols and a mace, burgesses and twelve freemen, its jurisdiction being a two-mile radius from St James' Church. The Market House was the administrative centre, presented to the Corporation by James I, and became the official residence for the Sovereign of Dingle. The Corporation held their meetings in the building and its dungeons were used as a jail.

In 1600 the 'Súgán' or pretender Earl of Desmond was refused admittance to the town by his relative, the Knight of Kerry, and in revenge he destroyed the town. The Dingle peninsula was the original county Kerry until joined by the rest of the county in 1606 after the Elizabethan troops under Colonel Ludlow sailed into Dingle Bay, where they landed their arms and supplies for raids throughout the county.

During the French Revolution, Count Rice of the Rice family of Dingle, who was serving in the French army, staged a plan to rescue Marie Antoinette from France and take her by ship to Dingle where she could go into hiding. The plan never materialised. Later, during the Penal days the priests had a Mass house in John Street when the local community came to celebrate the sacraments in secret. In 1793 many tenants rebelled against the excessive rents being charged. British troops were called in to quell a demonstration and they shot and killed fourteen of the demonstrators.

The Corporation built the pier in 1765 with a grant of £1,000. In later years the pier was extended. A linen industry developed significantly and there was a lucrative export trade of linen and agricultural produce. Wine, salt and coal were imported into the town. Dingle was also an ideal centre for smuggling, as the many bays and inlets indenting the coast line gave ample cover to the movement of illicit contraband, including spirits and silks. In Charles O'Brien's survey of Kerry in 1804 he reported that in the Dingle area approximately 120 boats and hookers were engaged in coastal trading in the summer, and in herring fishing from September. Up to the mid-1830s the road from Dingle to Tralee was in such a deplorable state that the mail was passed from hand to hand at the half-way point.

During the famine years the Dingle and Ventry Mission operated schemes for the relief of hardship amongst the poor of the district. In the famine of 1845 the Sisters of Presentation Convent also provided meals and comfort for the destitute. A temporary workhouse opened in 1848 and four years later a permanent workhouse and hospital were established in the town. Overlooking the bay is a tower known as Hussey's Folly, built by Edward Hussey in the 1840s to give employment to the poor during the famine. Lispole, Ventry and Dingle were all part of Dingle parish and the three churches were erected within a few years of one another. St Mary's Catholic Church in Green Street was built in 1865 with red sandstone quarried in Minard. Dingle continued as a borough until 1840 when it lost its Government status.

In 1884 the Tralee and Dingle Light Railway decided to build a line from

Tralee to Dingle. Services on the three-foot gauge, thirty-seven mile line began on 31 March 1891. The track had to make the steep ascent of the Slieve Mish Mountains with a branch line to Castlegregory. The line incurred heavy losses and its passenger service was discontinued on 17 April 1939. It continued as a cattle train until June 1953.

In the Dingle Commons there are several clochans. At Upper Main Street at the side of the road is an unmistakable boulder with cup marks, known as 'the Holy Stone'. To the west of the town at Milltown are three prostrate stones with prehistoric markings. On the western side of Dingle Bay is Burnham House (now Coláiste Íde), former home of the de Moleyns family (Lord Ventry), with three ogham stones in its vicinity. On Burnham Hill is Esk Tower, thirty-five feet tall, erected in 1847 by Rev. Charles Gayer, the Protestant curate. On a headland east of the town is the lighthouse, built in 1885 for £600.

In 1911 Desmond FitzGerald came to Dingle, originally to learn Irish, but he soon became involved in the Irish Volunteers and began to train local members. The British authorities were unhappy with his activities and in January 1915 he was instructed to leave the area within six days. He moved to Bray, County Wicklow and was later imprisoned in Mountjoy Jail. In the Cumann na nGaedheal Government of 1923 he was Minister of External

Affairs. On Easter Sunday 1916 plans were made that all Volunteer companies on the Dingle peninsula were to march into Tralee, but the order was cancelled. The police inspector at Dingle had responsibility for the barracks at Annascaul, Ballyferriter, Camp, Castlegregory and Cloghane, all of which were burned during the campaign of 1920.

With the release of David Lean's film, *Ryan's Daughter*, in 1970 the area was to enjoy a new prosperity, with the opening of many up-market restaurants and craft shops as the landscape and rugged beauty of the peninsula were exhibited to a world-wide audience through the film. Visitors sought out the beaches, glens and buildings where Robert Mitchum, Sarah Miles, John Mills and Trevor Howard had acted out the epic love story.

Combined with the scenery the three biggest attractions locally are the annual Regatta, the Races, and Fungie the dolphin. The first canoe regatta was held in Dingle in 1857 and the regattas proper commenced in the 1890s. The regatta, starting at the pier head each August, is a festive occasion and in recent years has been started by the former Taoiseach, Charles J. Haughey, who holidays on nearby Inishvickillaune. The Dingle Races, also held during August at Ballintaggart, are the biggest 'flapper' meeting in the country and attract horses from all over Ireland. The most unusual attraction of the area is Fungie the dolphin, who has lived in Dingle Bay since 1984 and performs to the delight of tourists.

RECOMMENDED

O'Flaherty's Pub, Bridge Street, for traditional music.

Café Liteartha, off Main Street. Bookshop and restaurant.

Tourist Office, Main Street, open during summer months.

St James' Church.

Máire de Barra's pub and restaurant.

Ceardlann Craft Village.

Fungie the dolphin.

Boats for hire on pier.

Dingle Races, mid-August.

Dingle Regatta, mid-August.

Simple Pleasures, The Mall, Antiques and Craft Gallery.

An Droichead Beag, Lower Main Street, traditional music.

Benners Hotel.

Skellig Hotel.

Sméara Dubha, Vegetarian Restaurant.

Hillgrove Hotel.

Cúl an Tí wholefood reataurant

Tom Long's Bar.

Fado Antiques.

Dingle courthouse and, inset, plaque on another house in Dingle to Jeremiah Curtin, 'Ethnologist, folklorist and well-known author. Born in the USA of Irish descent, he visited Ireland twice and stayed in this house in 1892. He collected stories here from local old people, and versions of these can be found in his books.'

Ventry

The village of Ventry is five miles west of Dingle, on the coast road to the picturesque Slea Head. Ventry (Fionn Tráigh, the Bright Strand or White Strand) Harbour is situated between two rocky headlands on Dingle Bay, each of which has a rath, with another in the centre. There is a Geraldine Castle at Rahinnane. Ventry parish, in Corca Dhuibhne barony, was composed of seventeen bailies.

This is the beginning of the Irish-speaking area of the Peninsula and you are liable to encounter children speaking Gaelic. On a hill to the right are holiday cottages and the Ventry Inn. A turn to the left leads to another long sandy beach and caravan park. This is much enjoyed by families and sailboarders. Further along the main road is a pottery shop and restaurant. This is a good place to stop for a meal or snack and to browse through the range of pottery. Some miles further on, Ventry Catholic Church stands at a crossroads opposite the pub owned by renowned footballer, Paudi O'Shea. This is the venue for great music sessions. Dolly Parton and Tom Cruise are among those who have visited the pub. Past Ventry are the Fahan group of clochans (beehive huts) and Dunbeg Fort.

Legends abound in the area. In Ventry Harbour the invading ships of Daire Donn, the King of the World who planned to invade and conquer Ireland, landed for his great battle with Fionn Mac Cumhail and his Fianna. The Fianna had mustered an army of nine thousand men and twelve thousand reserves and the battle raged for a year and a day. They engaged in single combat with swords and Daire Donn was killed. He was buried at Kilvickard-Owning, south of the village. The encounter became known as the Battle of Ventry Harbour.

During the Desmond Wars, Admiral Winter anchored his fleet here and gave shelter to refugees who were displaced from their dwellings. The land was granted to John Mullins, a Cromwellian officer who was paid in land for his services to the Crown. Later his family changed their name to de Moleyns and they built Burnham House as their family residence. In 1799 when the Act of Union was being negotiated Sir Thomas Mullins, who was knighted in 1797, was the only important Kerry landowner to profess anti-union sympathies. In return for an Irish peerage he agreed to bring his two sons as Unionists into the House of Commons. On 30 July 1800 Thomas Townsend Arembery Mullins, of Burnham House, was created Lord Ventry. He owned 100,000 acres of County Kerry which he let for £20,000 annual rent but many tenants were unable to keep up payments and only after much agitation and negotiation by Thomas O'Donnell, MP was the matter resolved. In 1837 a coastguard station was built but this was later abandoned, and a new one which was erected at Cuan was destroyed during the Anglo-Irish war.

On her *Rambles through Kerry* in 1839 Lady Chatterton wrote: 'The little fishing cove of Ventry is built on the high sandbank of a small bay, on the shores of which a few boats were lying, high and dry, and their owners were seen lingering lazily about them. It was however, a very picturesque little place, delightfully ragged and ruinous, suiting an artist exactly from the forlornness of its aspect. The bay, indeed, is good; and with its fine sands might be made a most attractive little bathing-place'.

Dunbeg fort

The Church of Ireland colony was established by the Dingle and Ventry Mission in 1840. An English rector, Charles Gayer, was in charge of the operation and received the full backing of Lord Ventry. He built a school house at Ventry and many people converted to Protestantism. It was the centre of the earliest attempts at proselytising in the west of Ireland and was successful. The mission did much to relieve the distress and hunger of the poor, particularly on the Blasket Islands. An Erasmus Smith school was later built on the site. The Catholic saint, St Kathleen is honoured in Ventry on her feast day, 25 November.

In their travel journal of 1840 Mr and Mrs S.C. Hall recorded: 'The houses about Ventry are generally neat, clean, and whitewashed; the smoke has chimneys to get out through, and the light has windows to get in at; and one at least of John Wesley's doctrines, that cleanliness is akin to godliness'.

In her book on Dingle written in 1846, Mrs D.P. Thompson gave her account of the village: 'Ventry, lying in the centre of the district (of Protestant missionary activity) became a gathering place and many converts from other parishes collected for strength and mutual support in this poor village which had been nearly depopulated by cholera'.

In 1850 the Bishop of Kerry confirmed eighty-six children in Ventry, but as he did not understand Irish and the children knew no English the questions had to be repeated by Mr Moriarty, their teacher, in their native tongue. A new Catholic Church was built in 1874.

Ventry is noted for its abundance of beehive type cells, ogham stones, souterrains and a cross. The Fahan group, three miles west of the village, holds the largest collection of beehive huts. To the west of the harbour is Mount Eagle, which has an abundance of ancient monuments. In the townland of Rahinaun (Ráth Fhionáin), a mile north of the strand, stands a castle of the Knight of Kerry. Dunbeg Fort (Dún Beag: the Small Fort) is a fortified triangular stone fort, overlooking the sea, west of Ventry.

This section of the peninsula has long been an Irish-speaking area and each year hundreds of students attend summer courses to perfect their native tongue.

RECOMMENDED

Pottery shop and restaurant.
Paudi O'Shea's Pub.
Beehive huts.
Dunbeg Fort.
Ventry Inn.

Dunquin

The village of Dunquin (Dún Chaoin, Pleasant Fort), is the main Irish-speaking area of the Dingle Peninsula. Dunquin lies between Clogher Head to the north, and Dunmore Head to the south which is the most westerly point on the mainland of Europe, facing the Atlantic Ocean.

Moving westwards along the coast from Ventry the road winds above steep cliffs and gives the first glimpse of the Blasket Islands. A short distance further on the traveller comes to Slea Head, with a viewing area of the islands and the breakers of Coomeenole Beach. At Dunmore Head the traveller should stop and walk out to the point, which is the most westerly headland in the country. Dunquin is a quaint Irish village with whitewashed cottages, turf reeks and stone walls. Park the car and walk the boreens, calling to Kruger Kavanagh's pub for a pint and music session. Louis Mulcahy's pottery shop has a wide range of quality pottery. During the summer season a ferry service leaves Dunquin pier for trips to the Great Blasket. On a headland to the north of the village is the school house which was built for *Ryan's Daughter*.

Dunquin is one of the oldest villages in Kerry and is first mentioned by the poet Mac Liag in the Book of Ballymote. Mac Liag was the chief poet of Brian Boru. The Annals of the Four Masters also mention it: 'The age of Christ, 1582 — at this period it was commonly said that the lowing of a cow or the voice of a ploughman could scarcely be heard from Dunquin to Cashel in Munster'.

At Dunquin harbour the cliffs consist of coloured Silurian rocks which date back more than four hundred million years. From Dunquin pier boats set out to the Blasket Islands and the rich fishing grounds off the islands. Today the boat passengers are mainly tourists visiting the Great Blasket. When the last islanders vacated the Blaskets in 1953 they settled in the Dunquin area, within sight of their former homes.

In 1830 there was a coastguard station at Ballyikeen, manned by men called Fir Ghorma, 'Blue Men', owing to the colour of their uniforms. Divine services were conducted in the coastguard station every Sunday by the vicar who received tithes of £75.

In 1837 Samuel Lewis wrote: 'The parish contains 4,937 statute acres, as applotted under the tithe set, of which nearly one half consists of coarse rocky mountain pasture, interspersed with patches of bog; the remainder is in tillage: sea-weed is extensively used for manure, and the state of agriculture is gradually improving'.

Following a visit in 1838 Lady Chatterton gave her impression of the village: 'Dunquin is a sad-looking village, on the western point of Europe, built near the edge of a precipitous cliff of dark sandstone, in which, as if worn away by the furious billows of the Atlantic, there are now several little caves, that serve the poor inhabitants to shelter their tiny fleet of fishing-boats'.

A small community once lived at Maum Clasach on the pass leading from the village to Ventry. There were over one hundred people living there in 1841 before the famine struck the district. Sadly the community did not survive, due to starvation and emigration, and a decade later the cabins lay

Top: Beehive huts, looking towards the Blasket islands
Below: house at Dunquin
Facing page: Village built for the film Far and Away

deserted. Dunquin Catholic Church was replaced by the parish priest, Fr Mangan, in 1857 with a new church in Ballintemple (Baile an Teampaill, the Village of the Church). The original thatched roof was later replaced by a wooden one, made from timber salvaged from the sea. Even by 1900 the roads were almost impassable for horses and carts, and donkeys were used to transport goods with baskets suspended from their backs.

One of the best-known landmarks in the village is Kruger's pub. The premises was once owned by a colourful character named Kruger Kavanagh. He was born in Dunquin in 1894 but spent a long time working in America. On returning to his native village he opened the pub which became renowned for its traditional music, sean-nós (old style) singing and set dancing. It was frequented by musicians, poets, singers and writers including Brendan Behan, Robert Bolt and Bryan MacMahon. Nearby is the new interpretive centre. Peig Sayers, who distinguished herself by writing a beautifully crafted book of life on the Blaskets, is buried in the small cemetery above the village.

In 1969 internationally acclaimed film director, David Lean, chose this area of the Dingle peninsula as the central location for his film, *Ryan's Daughter*. The multi-million dollar production, starring Robert Mitchum, Sarah Miles, John Mills, Trevor Howard, Leo McKern and a host of Irish character actors, was a love story set in an Irish village, against a backdrop of 'The Troubles'. Lean was meticulous in his filming of the spectacular storm sequence and his construction of a complete village above Dunquin for the film. The spin-off to local trade, industry and the hotel business was enormous and locals were hired by the score as extras. The film was a year in production and on its release tourists flocked to the area seeking out the locations and picturesque landscapes depicted in the film. *Ryan's Daughter* won two Academy Awards, one for John Mills's portrayal of the village idiot and a second for Freddie Young, director of photography. All that remains of the film set today is the school house.

In 1991 another entire village was constructed above Dunquin by film-makers. The film was the forty-million-dollar production, *Far and Away* starring Tom Cruise and Nicole Kidman and directed by Ron Howard. Cruise played Joseph Donnel, a young Connemara man who sets out in 1893 to avenge the death of his father, a tenant farmer who had fallen victim to a land owner, and is forced to emigrate to America. Local men grew beards and their hair long for parts as extras.

RECOMMENDED

Kruger Kavanagh's Pub.
Louis Mulcahy's Pottery Shop.
Peig Sayers' grave in Dunquin graveyard.
School house from Ryan's Daughter.
Dunquin Pier.
Dunmore Head.
Ferry to the Blaskets.

The Blaskets

The Blasket Islands are in the Atlantic Ocean, off-shore from Dunmore Head, at the south-western tip of the Dingle peninsula. The largest island, the Great Blasket, was inhabited by an Irish-speaking community until 1953. The five other islands are Inishvickillaune, Inis na Bro, Tearacht, Beiginis and Inis Tuaisceart. Proof of the island's ancient origins is provided by stone beehive huts and a small ring fort dating from the Iron Age. On the northern side of the Great Blasket is a thousand-foot high cliff, appropriately named Fatal Cliff.

There are magnificent views of the Blaskets from along the Slea Head road and particularly from Dunmore Head. Even if you suffer from sea-sickness, it's worth taking a boat trip from Dunquin Pier to the Great Blasket. During the summer months, boats commute between the mainland and island at regular intervals. The most suitable time for this trip is on a sunny day and remember to bring a picnic. Allow time to explore the island and examine the ring fort, beehive huts and remains of the houses.

Legal documents indicate that from the thirteenth century the Earl of Desmond leased the Great Blasket to the Ferriter family, who in turn paid two hawks as an annual rent. The Ferriters remained in possession until 1583 and the end of the Desmond rebellion. The British authorities then allocated the land to Protestant planters and eventually to two English adventurers, named Champion and Stone. Following various other transactions the Blaskets were taken over by Sir Richard Boyle. On maps of the sixteenth and seventeenth centuries the Blaskets are often referred to as 'Ferriter's Islands'. Ferriter's Castle was situated on a small headland known as Rinn a' Chaisleáin (Castle Point). Land close to the castle was used by islanders as an unconsecrated graveyard where shipwreck victims were buried.

In September 1588 a number of Spanish Armada galleons were blown ashore on the Blaskets and hundreds of lives were lost. The Prince of Ascule, son of the King of Spain, was lost when his ship, the *Santa Maria de la Rosa,* was wrecked amongst the islands. He was buried beside the old church of Dunquin. Spanish sailors who were saved were captured and taken to Dingle. Another Spanish ship which sank in the Sound was the *San Juan de Ragusa.*

During the mid-eighteenth century there was a small community living in cabins on the Great Blasket. During the great famine (1846-50) the population declined but not to the same degree as on the mainland. The Griffith Valuation Survey of the 1850s showed seventeen householders on the Great Blasket and one on Inishvickillaune. There were no occupants on the other islands. The main food of the islanders was fish and various forms of bird and wild life. Salvage from shipwrecks during the 1850s assisted considerably to ease the burden and was an incentive to the islanders to risk life and limb for their bounty. The Dingle and Ventry Protestant Mission also offered the poor relief during this period. Some people on the Great Blasket sent their children to the soup house. The soup house was administered by Protestants and they provided soup to those who attended their services. Many adults would not accept their terms for religious reasons but sent their starving children. When conditions improved they abandoned this practice.

Until 1907 the islands were part of the Cork and Orrery estate when the Great Blasket was purchased by the Congested Districts and tenants moved in.

BLASKET ISLAND

The curragh or naomhóg was the main mode of transport for islanders to the mainland. The curragh is a small boat made of tarred canvas stretched over a wooden frame.

The Great Blasket was noted for its many literary figures and three in particular capture its true character: Tomas Ó Criomhthain with his autobiography, *An tOileánach* (*The Islandman*), which gave a graphic description of the life and hardship of the island people; Muiris Ó Súilleabháin in *Fiche Bliain ag Fás (Twenty Years a-Growing)*, depicted his young life on the island; Peig Sayers' traditional lifestyle is simply described in her autobiography, *Peig*. All three wrote their books in Irish in the 1930s and their works were later translated into English.

On 17 November 1953 the last twenty-two of the islanders left the island on board the fishing boat, *St Lawrence O'Toole*, to start a new life on the mainland, within sight of their old homes.

On Inishvickillaune, the former Taoiseach, Charles J. Haughey, has built a house where he and his family frequently spend their holidays. On the island, St Brendan's Oratory, a small church and several clochans indicate the site of an early settlement.

RECOMMENDED

Ring fort.
Beehive huts.
Remains of houses from the first half of this century.

Ballyferriter

REASK
EARLY CHRISTIAN PILLAR

Ballyferriter, situated at the western end of the Dingle peninsula, is the largest village in the Gaeltacht area. The name Ballyferriter, Baile an Fheirtéaraigh, means 'the town of Ferriter'. The Ferriters were a Norman family who settled there in the thirteenth century and rented land from the Earl of Desmond. The best known of the Ferriter family was Piaras, a poet and rebel whom the Cromwellians hanged in Killarney in 1653.

The village is a suitable resting place to take a break on the circuit of the peninsula, particularly for cyclists. For its size Ballyferriter has an abundance of pubs where a drink or snack can be purchased. For those seeking a more substantial meal there is the nearby Dún an Óir Hotel, with its self-catering cottages and golf course, or the Granville Hotel. In Ballyferriter the Heritage Centre, facing the church, is worth a visit to gain a better understanding of the area, its culture and folklore. At night there are music sessions in many of the pubs. A few miles away, at Feothanach, is Teach Siamsa, a small theatre which presents traditional Irish evenings. There is a number of secluded beaches in the vicinity. Wine Strand is a popular safe beach. Within a short drive of the village are some historical and archaeological locations including Gallarus Castle and Oratory, the Reasc stone, Dún an Óir and Kilmalkedar Church.

At the southern side of Cape Sybil or Sybil Head, at the head of a small creek, was a castle called Sybilla's or Ferriter's Castle. Sybil Lynch was a seventeenth-century Galway girl who was in love with one of the Ferriters but her father disapproved of the relationship. The young couple decided to elope to Kerry but were pursued by her father and a small force. When the castle came under attack Ferriter hid Sybil in a cave under the castle. On putting the attackers to flight Ferriter returned to the cave to find that Sybil had drowned with the rising tide.

In 1569 James Fitzmaurice Fitzgerald organised a revolt against the Crown and asked the clergy and Catholic lords of Ireland to join in the defence of Munster. From the time of the Viking invasion Smerwick Harbour, close to Ballyferriter, was the main port of Kerry. On the north-west side of Smerwick harbour, near Drumlin Head, are the remains of a Spanish fortification called 'Fort-del-Ore' (Fort of Gold). In 1579 the Papal Nuncio, Dr Nicholas Sanders, and eighty Spaniards landed and built a fort on a rocky area jutting into the bay. James Fitzmaurice Fitzgerald, who supported the Spanish, left the fort to seek assistance from the Irish lords but none was forthcoming and he was killed. The following year, another force of six hundred men, consisting of Spanish, Basques and Italians, came to strengthen the fortress and establish a bridgehead for an invasion of Ireland.

On 7 November 1580 a strong English land force of at least eight hundred men and a naval fleet of six men-of-war under Lord Deputy Grey and Admiral Winter, attacked the fort. The occupants found it too difficult to defend and following a three-day siege the Italian commander, Sebastian San Guiseppe, surrendered to Grey, on condition that his garrison be spared. The men put down their arms and surrendered to the British but all the prisoners were put to the sword in cold blood in what became known as 'The Massacre of Smerwick Harbour'. Only the commander and officers were spared. Although Grey was widely criticised for his action, Queen Elizabeth I was pleased.

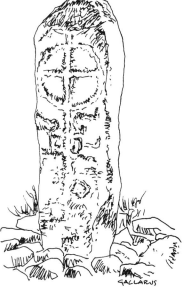

Gallarus oratory
Overleaf, top: Teach Siamsa at
Feothanach near Dingle,
and bottom: Kilmalkedar church

The building of the Catholic church in Ballyferriter was greatly assisted by donations from the poor in the parish. Work commenced on the building of the church in 1855. In 1880 a forty-foot watch tower was erected on Sybil Head as there was fear of a French invasion.

The Granville Hotel was originally built as a rectory, around 1830, in the Georgian style. From the turn of the century it was leased to the Royal Irish Constabulary and used as a barracks until 1922 when it was burned during the Civil War. Later it was bought by the Granville family who restored it and opened it as a hotel.

In August 1940 two IRA leaders, Frank Ryan and Sean Russell, travelled by U-boat from Smerwick Harbour for Germany. Russell died on the voyage and Ryan continued to Germany.

Ballyferriter is the headquarters of Comharchumann Forbartha Chorca Dhuibhne (a local co-operative founded in 1967). The old school house now houses a Heritage Centre and coffee shop. Radio na Gaeltachta, the Irish language radio station, is situated close to the small fishing village of Ballydavid. From Ballydavid there is a clifftop path which extends to Brandon Creek, the location from which St Brendan is believed to have set sail for the New World. In 1976, the explorer Tim Severin headed an expedition which sailed from here in a replica boat and re-enacted the voyage of St Brendan to America.

Within a few miles of Ballyferriter there are several historical sites. Reask Slab Cross, with its unique design, is in the setting of an early monastic settlement, containing an oratory, graves, clochauns and cross-inscribed pillars and slabs. Some of these were excavated during the 1970s.

Gallarus Oratory overlooks Smerwick Harbour in what was once a large Christian settlement. It dates to the seventh century and is the best preserved early Christian church building in Ireland. The structure was built of unmortared stone and is still waterproof. Locals now request payment for parking in a field adjoining Gallarus Oratory, for which there is no entry charge. Nearby is the four storey Gallarus Castle, once owned by the Fitzgeralds, where a fifteenth-century Knight of Kerry once resided. English troops were garrisoned there during the siege of Fort-del-Ore. In 1622 Maurice Fitzgerald found it necessary to sell off part of the land of Gallarus.

This area is steeped in legend and folklore. Close by are the remains of Kilmalkedar Church, where St Maolcheadar built a church around 600 AD. He died there in 636 AD. The church has an Irish-Romanesque doorway and legend has it that if you pass through the East Window (Cró na Snáthaide) you will go to heaven. In the church grounds are the famous ogham 'alphabet' stone, a sundial and some ancient tombs. Near the church is the thirteenth century St Brendan's house.

SUN-DIAL (SE FACE)
KILMALKEDAR

RECOMMENDED

Ferriter's Castle.

Reasc Cross.

Gallarus Castle.

Gallarus Oratory.

Kilmalkedar Church.

Wine Strand.

Granville Hotel.

Teach Siamsa.

Heritage Centre.

Dun an Óir Hotel and golf course.

Tigh Pheig, traditional music.

Murphy's pub, traditional music.

BALLYFERRITER

Lispole

The village of Lispole, Lios Póil (Paul's Ring Fort), is east of Dingle. Lispole railway station (now closed down) is in the barony of Corcaguiney. North of the station is the medieval St Martin's church in the graveyard. Up to 1817 Lispole was part of Annascaul parish when Bishop Sugrue of Kerry made it part of Dingle parish. The old church, built in 1710, was a long low thatched building. On 28 August 1867 a new church was opened on the occasion of the Pattern in Minard. Around this time new churches were also built in Dingle and Ventry. A traveller can also trace the course of the old Tralee-Dingle railway line through the district.

North of Lispole village is a large earthen fort in the midst of which are the ruins of Teampall Liath (the Grey Church) dedicated to St Martin, and further on in the townland of Aughacarrible (Ath an Charbaid, the Fort of the Chariot) is a large boulder inscribed with four sets of concentric circles together with smaller counterparts and a number of cup-marks. In the nearby village of Furacht, on a hill to the east, is a carved stone. There are also two cups and circle stones, an ogham stone and holy wells, dedicated to Our Lady, St Fionán and St Michael. Further west at Kinard, near the burial ground, is an ogham stone.

Three miles south of Lispole is Minard Castle which was built by the Knight of Kerry in 1560. Walter Hussey later took charge of the castle and was killed when it was attacked by Cromwellian forces under Sadler and Le Hunt in 1650. The small beach beneath the castle has an abundance of red sandstone boulders which are of geological interest. Stone was quarried from this location for many buildings. Close to the castle is the site of the old church of St Mary. It was from this church that the townland got its name — Kilmurray; Cill Muire, built by the Geraldines at the beginning of the fourteenth century. The ruins of the castle featured in David Lean's film *Ryan's Daughter*.

Thomas Ashe, the patriot, was born in Kinard on 12 January 1885, the son of a comfortable farmer. He became a teacher in North Dublin and a member of the Gaelic League. Early in 1916 he was appointed commandant of the Fifth Battalion of the Fingal Brigade, IRA and led a successful action against the RIC barracks at Ashbourne, County Meath. When Ashe and a colleague, Timothy Brosnan, travelled home to Lispole by motorcar in June 1916 they were given an enthusiastic reception. In August 1917 Ashe was arrested and went on hunger strike in Mountjoy Jail but was forcibly fed before he died on 25 September 1917.

A Celtic cross monument has been erected to Lieutenant T.M. Ashe, Lieutenant T. Hawley and M. Fitzgerald, members of C Company (Lispole) Fifth Battalion, killed in action at Lispole ambush on 21 March 1921.

RECOMMENDED

Temple Martin Church.
Minard Castle.
Old railway line.
Monument to Ambush victims.

MINARD CASTLE

... A FORD OF HEROES, EXPLORERS, SCULPTORS ...

Annascaul

The quiet village of Annascaul, a farming community on the Owenascaul River, is situated in the heart of the Dingle peninsula. The name Annascaul (Áth na Scál), Ford of the Heroes, is said to come from Scál ní Mhurnáin who featured in another Cuchulainn legend. A giant tried to take Scál but Cuchulainn came to her rescue. From opposite sides of the lake they threw boulders at each other. Cuchulainn was struck and injured and Scál, fearing him dead, drowned herself in the lake which was named after her. The village consists of a long main street with shops and houses set well back from the road.

At this juncture several detours are recommended. One southwards will take you to Inch Strand where swimming and sailboarding can be enjoyed. Two miles north of the village, a winding road will take you on a mountain path alongside Annascaul lake, affording some magnificent views.

On Dromavally Mountain there are three stone cairns. Tradition states that the location had associations with Cuchulainn and some refer to it as 'Cuchulainn's Castle'. Nearby is Coomduv Lake, and at nearby Knockane stands a rock inscribed with a chi-rho cross (style of cross which signifies Christ: the style dates to fifth-century Gaul). In the vicinity there are several ogham stones, at Ballintermon, Ballinhunt and beside an ancient church at Ballinvohor. The holy well of St John the Baptist is nearby at Ballinclare. There are many souterrains (underground passages) in the area.

By the early 1800s the village was on the main road and there was a receiving house for letters to and from Tralee and Dingle. The village had a police station and petty sessions were held on alternate Mondays. Five fairs were held annually.

In 1837 Samuel Lewis wrote: 'The parish church, a small plain edifice with a square tower, is situated here: and a Roman Catholic chapel has been erected. In the vicinity is a "beautiful lake" about a mile in circumference; and in a glen among the mountains in its neighbourhood, bordering on Ballyduff, it is said the last wolf in Ireland was killed: the particular spot is called "Wolf Step".'

A notable landmark at the western end of the village is the South Pole Inn in which Tom Crean lived following his return from Captain Scott's expedition to the South Pole. Crean was born in Annascaul in 1877 and enlisted in the Royal Navy in 1893 as a Boy Second Class. Crean's heroic deed of going for help for his colleagues on Elephant Island is still remembered. There are many souvenirs from his expeditions in the building, including his Albert Award and a set of silver from Ernest Shackleton. Tom Crean died on 27 July 1938 and was buried in Ballinacourty, near the village. Another pub worth a visit is Dan Foley's.

A few miles east of the village is the famed Inch Strand, which extends five miles into the sea. The strand was used as the central location for the screen adaptation of John Millington Synge's classic play, *The Playboy of the Western World*, directed by Brian Desmond Hurst with Siobhan McKenna as Pegeen Mike and Gary Raymond as Christy Mahon. Many travellers and locals were employed as extras on the film.

Another prominent local figure was Jerome Connor, the Irish sculptor. He

INCH

was born in Coumduff, Annascaul in 1876, the sixth child of a small farmer. When Jerome was fourteen, the family emigrated to America and settled in Massachusetts. He became a stone mason and began sculpting busts and Civil War monuments. By the time he returned to live in Dublin in 1925, he had gained quite a reputation. Among his works are Robert Emmet memorials in St Stephen's Green, Dublin and the Smithsonian Institute in Washington, the *Lusitania* Monument, Cobh, and *Eire* in Merrion Square, Dublin. He died in poverty in 1943.

Close to Inch strand, on the main road to Dingle, is Red Cliff House, for many years the summer residence of the Bishop of Kerry. Bishop Eamonn Casey resided here while Bishop of Kerry (1969–76). In 1974, he commenced his affair with Annie Murphy here, resulting in the birth of their son Peter, and in Dr Casey's resignation as Bishop of Galway in 1992.

RECOMMENDED

South Pole Inn.
Inch Strand.
Coomduv Lake.
Dan Foley's Pub.
The Bog View Hostel.
Blackluin House.

. . . A CLUSTER OF HOUSES, SOME PUBS AND A CHURCH . . .

Camp

Travelling northwards from Annascaul the traveller will reach the small village of Camp, which is merely a cluster of houses, some pubs and a church. The name in Irish is An Cam, meaning the Hollow, which describes its position at the western side of the Slieve Mish Mountains. It is a good starting point to explore the highest peaks of Caherconree (stone fort), at 2,713 feet, and to discover the ogham stones in the locality. The area is rich in history, legend and folklore. Taking a left turn the traveller will reach Naisi's Grave, the lover of Deirdre. Other stories relate how Cúraí MacDaire, High King of Munster, had his stronghold on the mountain. Cúraí and Cuchulainn engaged in a savage fight for the love of Blaithnaid at Caherconree, resulting in the death of Cúraí.

Two miles from Camp is Gleann na nGealt (Glen of the Madmen), so called because of a healing well which is reputed to have a cure for madness. Tradition has it that Gall, son of the Ulster King Fiachra, went mad after the Battle of Ventry and sought refuge in the glen. Three miles from the village is Killelton Oratory, a seventh-century Christian church. It is reputed that Fas, a legendary Milesian princess, is buried under the church. Close by are the remains of the ruined village of Killelton which was inhabited until the nineteenth century when the families were evicted.

Below the village at Curraduff there is a viaduct over the Finglas River on which the Tralee-Dingle railway line passed. On Whit Monday 1893 the Dingle train was travelling down towards Camp when it ran out of control and crashed over the viaduct, killing three crew and ninety pigs, and injuring thirteen passengers.

There has long been a tradition of sheep farming in Camp. From the early 1900s Lord Ventry ran a successful hill farm at Beheenagh with over a thousand head of sheep. In 1991 Jimmy O'Dwyer of Camp Cross won the Irish, English and Welsh record for shearing 520 sheep in nine hours. Every September there is a sheep fair in Camp.

Camp has produced a long list of outstanding GAA footballers. Thirty All-Ireland medals have been won by locals. In 1929 Tim O'Donnell brought the first All-Ireland medal to Camp.

There are good facilities in the village for horse-drawn caravans. The traveller seeking a break can decide between Ashe's and Daly's Bar.

Mike and Mary Fitzgerald preserve railway mementoes at their pub in Camp, also known as Paddy Joe's

RECOMMENDED

Naisi's Grave.
Shore Acre Caravan Park.
The Railway Tavern, Camp Junction.
Daly's Bar.
James Ashe's Bar.
Seaside Caravan Park, Camp.
Caherconree.
Killelton Oratory.

North Kerry

NORTH KERRY, IN CONTRAST to the peninsulas and southern portion of the county, consists chiefly of flat fertile farmland. What the area lacks in the rugged beauty of Killarney and Dingle is compensated for by the tranquillity of the villages. Many towns still retain their traditional appearance and have not succumbed to commercialism. The area is bordered by the Shannon estuary on the north, County Limerick on the east and westwards the beaches and cliffs of the Atlantic. Here and there you may still see milk churns being transported to the creamery by donkey and cart or tractor. Be patient when you have to drive behind one on a narrow road!

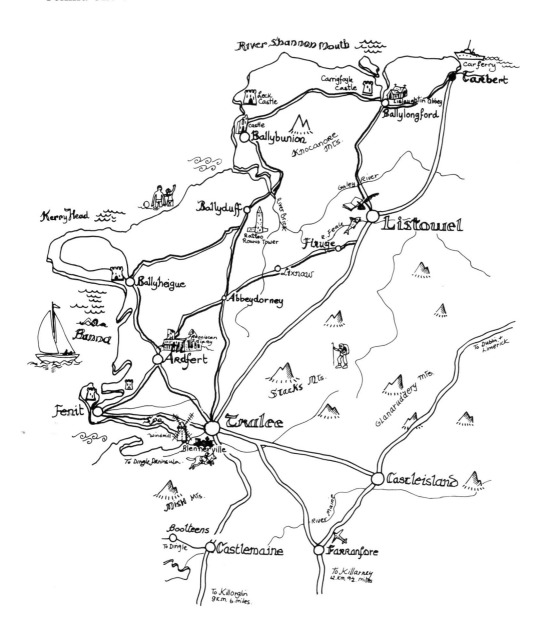

... WHERE TRAVELLERS CAN QUENCH THEIR THIRST ...

Tarbert

Tarbert is a small quiet village in North Kerry, shaped like the letter 'T', overlooking the River Shannon and the Hills of Clare. The Irish name is Tairbeart which means isthmus or peninsula but an older name for the village was Kilnaughtin. The name was also spelt as Terbot, Terbet and Terbart. The Down Survey referred to the district as 'Terbet West' and 'Terbet East.'

Approaching County Kerry on the coast road from Limerick, follow the road running parallel to the Shannon. At many points along the road the wide expanse of the Shannon can be seen. On leaving the village of Glin you will cross the northern boundary into County Kerry at Tarbert. An important feature of the village is the Tarbert-Killimer Car Ferry. There is an active branch of Comhaltas Ceoltóirí Éireann in the village and the Kerry Fleadh Cheoil (music festival) has been held here. There are several pubs in the village where travellers can quench their thirst. I can recall an enjoyable few hours of music, song, poetry and ham sandwiches in the Shannon Bar during a Writers' Week Literary Tour.

The first Lord Tarbert was Dermot O'Connor, whose family founded Lislaughtin Abbey. He divided his property between his three sons; Knockanure to Donough, Murher to Owen and Kilnaughtin to Tadhg, who became the second Lord Tarbert. Following the Elizabethan conquest the confiscated lands of the Earl of Desmond were divided out to planters who undertook to place English families on the land. Sir John Hollis was granted lands in Tarbert but refused to 'undertake'. Patrick Crosbie was granted the lands of Tarbert in order to plant the O'Moore septs of Laois. Later Crosbie's son sold some of the lands to Dominick Óg Roche, who was appointed Baron of Tramore by James I.

TARBERT C. of I 1814

Tarbert Bridewell

Construction of Tarbert House, the oldest inhabited house in Munster, built in Queen Anne style, commenced in 1690 but was not completed until 1720. The house was in the possession of the Leslie family who were of Hungarian origin and were descendants of Attila the Hun. They came to Ireland from Scotland in the fourteenth century and first settled in Sligo. Later they moved to Munster and in 1722 James Leslie was appointed high-sheriff of Kerry. The Leslie family still lives in Terbart House. The origins of Tarbert village owe much to the Leslies who developed it greatly from the mid-1700s. On Massy's Hill there is a seventeenth-century fort.

In *A Tour in Ireland* in 1779 Arthur Young wrote: 'The state of the poor is something better than it was twenty years ago, particularly their clothing, cattle and cabins. They live upon potatoes and milk; all have cows; and when they dry them, buy others. They also have butter, and most of them keep pigs, killing them for their own use.' Around this time there were about one hundred boats employed on the Shannon, fishing and bringing turf to Limerick from Kerry and Clare. Each boat was manned by two men and a boy.

Sixty-three years later William Makepeace Thackeray gave his observation of the place. 'The town of Tarbert, in the guide books and topographical dictionaries, flourishes considerably. You read of its port, its corn and provision stores. The town, in fact, contains about a dozen of houses, some hundreds of cabins, and two hotels.'

The Erasmus Smith school opened in 1790 and in 1940 it became the site for St Ita's College. During the nineteenth century Tarbert was to develop considerably, with the Protestant Kilnaughtin church being built on Steeple Road in 1830. Three years later St Mary's Catholic church was erected in Chapel Street for the sum of £1,200. The Gothic structure of the Church of Ireland at Tieraclea was built in 1814. There was also a Wesleyan church in Church Street. The stone Bridewell built in 1831 on Island Road was used as a local courthouse and jail for over a century. The magistrates were members of the Leslie family. John Redmond, the Irish Parliamentary Party MP, supported the local leadership of the Irish Land League during the Land War.

The village was to take advantage of its situation on the Shannon and it became a busy port exporting corn, grain and agricultural produce while salt, coal and other merchandise were imported. Other maritime projects undertaken included the erection of a coastguard station and lighthouse: work commenced in 1831 and was completed in March 1834. Tarbert was part of the Ballylongford/Tarbert parish until 1859 when it became a parish in its own right.

Located on a rock on the north east side of Tarbert Island, the lighthouse stands seventy-five feet high and 170 feet in circumference. The stone used in its manufacture came from Cornwall and it was reported that five men lost their lives transferring it ashore. In March 1867 the gunboat *Hind* proceeded to Tarbert to reinforce the coastguard ship *Frederick William*. The coming of the railway was to have a detrimental effect on Tarbert as a port as the shipping of goods through Tarbert Island greatly diminished.

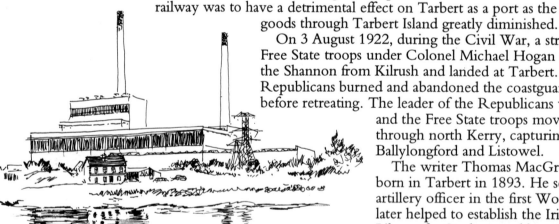

TARBERT
ESB & SHANNON BAR

On 3 August 1922, during the Civil War, a strong force of Free State troops under Colonel Michael Hogan sailed across the Shannon from Kilrush and landed at Tarbert. The Republicans burned and abandoned the coastguard station before retreating. The leader of the Republicans was captured and the Free State troops moved on through north Kerry, capturing Ballylongford and Listowel.

The writer Thomas MacGreevy was born in Tarbert in 1893. He served as an artillery officer in the first World War and later helped to establish the Irish Central Library for Students and became an arts journalist. He was a close friend of Samuel Beckett, Jack B. Yeats and James Joyce; he was with the latter when he died and became executor of his will. Amongst his works are *Introduction to the Method of Leonardo da Vinci* and *Collected Poems*. A plaque to his memory was erected on the house where he was born.

In 1968 the ESB established an electricity generating station on each side of the Shannon, one being in Tarbert. They are easily distinguishable by their twin chimneys. A car ferry linking Tarbert across the Shannon to Killimer in County Clare opened in May 1969. A traveller intending to go from Kerry to Clare can avoid Limerick city by taking the ferry. The MV *Shannon Willow* carries forty-four cars and operates all year round.

RECOMMENDED

The Car Ferry.

Thomas MacGreevy's house.

Tarbert House.

Shannon Bar.

Tarbert Island Regatta, end June.

... BY THE GIANT'S GRAVE, A QUIET, SLEEPY VILLAGE ...

Ballylongford

Ballylongford is situated in North Kerry, at the head of a creek on the River Shannon estuary. The name in Irish is Béal Átha Longfoirt (the Mouth of the Ford of the Fortress) which originally applied to the ford over the little river before the erection of the bridge. The ancestral lands of the O'Connor Kerry family included in the barony of Iraghticonnor were situated between the opposing forces of the Knight of Glin and Lord Fitzmaurice. In 1478 John O'Connor Kerry founded Lislaughtin Friary for the Franciscans of the Strict Observance on the site of an ancient monastery, founded by St Lachtin.

Ballylongford is another quiet sleepy village with its quota of pubs and shops. One pub worth a visit is Kennelly's which is where the poet Brendan Kennelly was born. Recently the Ballylongford Regatta Club built a new club house at Saleen Pier. The annual Regatta is held in mid-July. South of Ballylongford, in Ballyline, is a chamber tomb known as the Giant's Grave.

Northwest of the village, close to the road from Ballybunion, is Carrigafoyle Castle, Carraig an Phoill (the Rock of the Hole), built in 1490 by Conor Liath O'Connor Kerry. The castle, the main stronghold of the family, had an eighty-six-foot tower and was completely surrounded by water giving it a strategic defensive location. From here O'Connor Kerry prevented ships proceeding up river to Limerick and confiscated some of their cargoes. During

the Desmond wars, in 1580, the castle came under fire from English naval artillery on sea and land, under the command of Sir William Pelham. Following a two-day siege the castle was taken and all the occupants, comprising nineteen Spanish and fifty Irish, under the command of an Italian engineer named Captain Julio, were hanged. At the same time Lislaughtin Friary was destroyed. After another battle in 1600 Lord President Carew took charge of the castle. A year later O'Connor Kerry recaptured it with the assistance of the Spanish and killed the English garrison. Cromwell's forces finally destroyed the castle and hanged the survivors in 1649.

In the late eighteenth century the conditions of the poor in Ballylongford were so bad that they were forced to eat seaweed and nettles, although by 1837 Samuel Lewis was to observe that the village had three hundred houses and an export business of turf and corn. In 1842 William Makepeace Thackeray was not so flattering and wrote: 'The cabins along the road were not much better than those to be seen south of Tralee, but the people were far better clothed, and indulged in several places in the luxury of pigsties.' On the nearby Carrig Island are the remains of an ancient church.

Below: A local pub at Astee, where Jesse James' father was born, and bottom: at Ballylongford a plaque commemorates the O'Rahilly, killed during the Easter Rising, 1916. Right and facing page: Lislaughtin Abbey, Ballylongford.

Due to its coastal location Ballylongford became a flashpoint during the Civil War and War of Independence. The O'Rahilly, who was born here in 1875, played an important part in the foundation of the Irish Volunteers and Sinn Féin. He organised the meeting at which the Irish Volunteers were formed in November 1913. In July 1914 he was at Howth to receive guns from Germany on board the *Asgard*. He was editor of *An Claidheamh Soluis*, a nationalist paper, and supported MacNeill's efforts to stop the Rising, travelling to Kerry with orders of cancellation. When the Rising finally broke out he headed back to Dublin and joined Pearse and Connolly in the GPO. During the insurrection he was shot and killed in Moore Street. A plaque has been erected on the house in which he was born in Ballylongford.

In January 1920 the Ballylongford company of the Volunteers wounded a policeman, and there followed a good deal of unrest with shootings and buildings being burned. That November, in a shoot-out between the IRA and Black and Tans, Edward Carmody, a local man, was shot dead. That same year several RIC constables resigned at the barracks. On 22 February 1921, the local IRA column planned an attack on the British in the village and ambushed a Black and Tan patrol, killing one and wounding another. In a reprisal the following day a force of Black and Tans entered the village and burned about twenty houses.

Brendan Kennelly was born in the village on 17 April 1936. He has gone on to become Professor of Modern Literature at Trinity College, Dublin and one of the country's most respected poets, with books such as *Cast a Cold Eye* and *Cromwell* to his credit. Another man of letters, Fr F.X. Martin, OSA was born in Ballylongford on 2 October 1922. He became Professor of Medieval History in University College, Dublin and is the author of many books including *The Irish Volunteers*, *The Course of Irish History* and *The Howth Gun-Running*. He won prominence and respect as a national figure in the 1970s as one of the main organisers in the (regrettably unsuccessful) campaign to save Wood Quay, a major international Viking site in Dublin from development as city offices.

RECOMMENDED

Ruins of Lislaughtin Abbey, half a mile north of the village.

Carrigfoyle Castle, also north of the village.

Beal Castle, north off the main road to Ballybunion.

Ballylongford Regatta.

Ballybunion

Ballybunion, situated eight miles west of Listowel, is one of the most popular seaside resorts on the west coast. The name of the town in Irish, Baile an Bhuinneanaigh (town of the Bunyans or Bunions), derives from the Bunyan family, retainers of the Geraldines.

It is a holiday town dependent on tourists for its survival. The great tourist boom of the 40s and 50s might be over, with Spain and the Canary Islands more attractive destinations, yet the resort swells during the summer months as holiday makers fill the hotels, guest houses, chalets and caravan parks. The town has a lively atmosphere with amusement arcades, a carnival, discos, fast food outlets and pubs, and offers an ideal family holiday. The fine beach is suitable for bathing and surfing. The resort is affectionately known as 'Ballybee'. One of the highlights of the year is the International Bachelor Festival at the end of June.

Ballybunion Castle was built in the late thirteenth century for the Fitzmaurices at an elevated point above the cliffs. Thereafter it became the seat of the heirs of that family. It was captured in the Desmond wars and was confiscated along with the lands of William Óg Bunion in 1582. The castle and lands were first given to Edmond Barrett and in 1612 to Lord Kerry. In 1783 Richard Hare became owner of the castle and manor of Ballybunion. The castle still stands today, and has been the responsibility of the Office of Public Works since 1923.

Extensive cliffs extend in both directions from the castle. The area is noted for its caves, one of which is named the Seven Sisters. The cave derived its name from a legend which stated that seven daughters of a local chieftain tried to elope with his prisoners, seven Vikings. On being discovered, their father had them thrown through the roof into the cave. Another well-known local landmark is eight-hundred-foot Knockanure which comes from Cnoc an Áir, the hill of the killing, where Fionn Mac Cumhail and the Fianna attempted to defend a princess fleeing from pursuers. Another source suggests that it is Cnoc an Fhómhair, the hill of the harvest, where people took offerings of farm produce, or Cnoc an Iubhair, the hill of the yew tree.

Leck Castle, a stronghold of the Fitzgeralds, Earls of Desmond, sited above the cliffs was built in the 1380s. The heir to Leck Castle was killed with O'Connor Kerry in 1568 at the Battle of Lixnaw. In 1641 the castle was captured and the demesne granted to Trinity College, Dublin. In 1842 the castle was visited and favourably written about by the poet, Alfred Lord Tennyson.

Another Fitzmaurice stronghold, from the thirteenth century, was Beal Castle, five miles from Ballybunion. In August 1600 Lady Kerry ordered the murder of Maurice Stack, a renegade Kerryman, an accomplice of the land grabbers Richard Boyle, later Earl of Cork, and Sir Patrick Crosbie. Her husband,

in showing support for the action, hanged Stack's brother in another castle the following day. In 1783 Beal Castle moved into the control of Richard Hoare. Doon Castle was erected at Doon Point.

At the beginning of the nineteenth century there was great poverty in the area. In 1818 Fr McCarthy, the parish priest, called to each farmer in the parish and collected potatoes for the poor. From the early 1800s Ballybunion became a popular seaside resort and holiday-makers travelled there from all over Kerry, Clare and Limerick. There was a spin-off in employment with the construction of a hotel and guest houses to cater for the influx of visitors. At the time the town consisted chiefly of a long street with the hotel, shops, pubs and a police barracks.

In 1837 Samuel Lewis recorded his views of a visit to Ballybunion: 'This village ... has recently become a place of resort for sea-bathing, and is much frequented on account of the highly interesting and romantic caverns with which its cliffs are indented.'

Hall's Ireland of 1840 stated: 'The caves of Ballybunion are not often visited, yet they may be classed among the most remarkable of the natural wonders of Ireland. They are distinguished by names, each name bearing reference to some particular circumstance, as for example the Hunter's Path, from the tradition that a rider once rode his horse over it; Smuggler's Bay which, for centuries, was famous as a safe shelter for free traders.'

There was a strictly enforced rule of 'Men's' and 'Women's' beaches. At the annual September fair people gathered from the surrounding districts to sell their wares. The parish priest of Ballybunion led a group of enthusiastic locals in the promotion of building a railway line from Ballybunion to Listowel. After many plans were considered and found to be too expensive, the Listowel and Ballybunion Railway Act of 1886 agreed to the building of the Lartigue railway system for £33,000. It was a unique system which used a running rail mounted 3'4" above the ground and a series of trestles. The locomotive was built in Belgium. It was the first such line in Ireland and passenger services commenced on 29 February 1888. Initially, the line was profitable.

Thereafter, with better transportation and the large influx of tourists, there was rapid growth and development in the area. Permission was sought to acquire the foreshore and sand-dunes to run a second line adjacent to the shore but it never materialised. The Catholic church was built in 1897. In 1912 one of the first Marconi wireless stations was erected in Ballybunion and the voice of his engineer, W.T. Ditcham, was the first European voice heard by radio in America. The station operated until 1920.

In July 1916 the Ballybunion Volunteers marched to the RIC barracks and when stones were thrown at the building the RIC opened fire. Daniel Scanlon, a local man, was hit and later died. He became the first Volunteer casualty in North Kerry. On 22 February 1920 the local column of the IRA staged an attack on the Black and Tans but the attack failed and there were no casualties. The Castle Hotel, which was used by the British Army, was subsequently burned. Much of the rolling stock of the Lartigue railway was destroyed during the War of Independence and it finally closed on 14 October 1924.

Today Ballybunion is noted for its famed golf course. There are fears for the future of the course as it suffers annually from coastal erosion. It is still a popular resort, with emphasis now on discos, amusement arcades and caravan parks.

RECOMMENDED

The 18 hole golf course.

Fitzmaurice Castle, overlooking the beach.

Leck Castle, north of the town.

Several caravan parks with good facilities.

Ballybunion International Bachelor Festival, end June.

Liston's Bar, traditional music.

... A MARKET TOWN, AND THE KINGDOM'S LITERARY CAPITAL ...

Listowel

The market town of Listowel in north Kerry is situated on the banks of the River Feale. The name Listowel comes from the Irish, Lios Tuathail, the fort of Tuathal or O'Toole. Listowel appears in various forms from the early 1300s including Lystothyl, Listuoli and Listwohill.

There are numerous approach roads to the town of Listowel. Approaching the town from the Abbeyfeale road, a motorist passes close to the major Kerry Co-op complex, one of the most successful co-ops in the country. Entering the broad town square, you will see the Catholic church on the right and St John's church in the centre of the square. This latter building is now an Arts and Heritage Centre and Tourist Office. The Listowel Arms Hotel fits snugly into the corner close to the fifteenth-century castle. The town is noted for its fifty-odd pubs and the warm hand of friendship extended to strangers, especially those seeking their roots in the vicinity. The town has changed little in character and appearance in several generations. A comparison with a Lawrence photograph of the square of the 1880s shows that only the dress style and transportation have changed. A stroll around the town reveals a wide range of traditional shop and pub fronts.

In 1551 King Edward VI appointed the sixteenth Lord Kerry as Lord of Kerry and Captain of his Nation. In the fifteenth century the Lord of Kerry built Listowel Castle. It was the last stronghold to resist the Elizabethan forces during the Desmond revolt. On 2 December 1600, during the O'Neill campaign, Sir Charles Wilmot obtained Sir George Carew's approval to attack the castle. Following a prolonged siege, surviving members of the garrison surrendered and were either hanged, or put to the sword. Fr Dermot McBrodie carried Lord Kerry's eldest son, only five years old, to safety. After the destruction of the castle the town began to develop with the erection of some small cabins. In 1641 Lord Kerry was appointed Governor of Kerry. A Dominican priest was killed during the Williamite wars of 1691 as the English regained control of the county.

THE CASTLE
LISTOWEL

There was a very contrasting lifestyle for the poor and gentry of the area. In 1779 Arthur Young reported that the poor in Listowel lived on potatoes and milk. Yet the Right Honourable John Fitzmaurice, High Sheriff of County Kerry, was able to receive the judges of assize in style at the boundary of the county. Dressed in scarlet, he rode a horse with a Turkish bridle and was preceded by two running footmen. Then came four grooms and a dozen liverymen in the colours of the family. Following this procession rode the gentlemen of the county and all retired to a banquet of one hundred and twenty dishes in

Writer Bryan MacMahon, poet Gabriel Fitzmaurice and Arthur Flynn during Listowel Writers' Week

Listowel. Having travelled through torrential rain and heavy mud, the group were about to sit down to their banquet when word came through that the River Feale was rising, and as there were no bridges they had to depart urgently while the river was still fordable.

The Hare family bore the title Earl of Listowel. In 1783 Richard Hare, a Cork businessman, purchased the Earl of Kerry's local property. Hare and his son were returned as members of the Irish Parliament and voted for the Union. He became Baron Ennismore in 1800, Viscount Ennismore and Listowel in 1816 and in 1822 Earl of Listowel.

In 1814 Lord Listowel made a grant of two sites for a Catholic and a Protestant church in the town square. Five years later the Protestants began building their church which was named St John's. (Today it is an Arts Centre). The Catholic church began a decade later and replaced a temporary structure. In later years the spire and aisles were added. Following the famine of 1821 the Government promoted the building of roads. Limestone quarries were opened to construct the Listowel to Newcastlewest road. The bridge was built for £2,500 in 1829 by Richard Griffith.

William Makepeace Thackeray gave his opinion of Listowel in 1842: 'The place seemed like a scene at a country theatre, once smartly painted by the artist; but the paint has cracked in many places, the lines are worn away, and the whole piece only looks more shabby for the flaunting strokes of the brush which remain. And here, of course, came the usual crowd of idlers round the car: the epileptic idiot holding piteously out his empty tin snuff-box; the brutal idiot in an old soldier's coat, proffering his money-box, and grinning and clattering the single halfpenny it contained; the old man with no eyelids, calling upon you in the name of the Lord; the woman with a child at her hideous breast; the children without number.'

The Lartigue monorail was opened on 29 February 1888, the Jubilee year of Queen Victoria, and ran from Listowel to Ballybunion. A Spanish engineer, Charles Lartigue, constructed the railway on the principle of pannier-backs balanced on a donkey's back. The train was driven by a double boiler locomotive. It ran on an elevated V-shaped rail, with the windows facing outwards. Balance was most important and sacks of sand were available to this end.

George Hewson agreed to allow the company to draw as much sand as it required from the seashore on his estate for one penny per ton of sand. In 1883 a group of residents had petitioned for a tramway but it did not materialise. Work commenced on the Lartigue in late 1887 and was completed five months later at a cost of £33,000. The first train of eight carriages carried over one hundred passengers, including Lord Ventry and Lord Bessborough and representatives of the French Government. The last train ran on 14 October 1924.

BIRTHPLACE OF
MAURICE WALSH AUTHOR
1879 – 1964
ERECTED BY
WRITERS WEEK LISTOWEL

AND BALLYDONOGHUE
MAGAZINE COMMITTEE
3RD JUNE 1989

Charles Stewart Parnell made several appearances in Listowel. In his last public meeting he addressed a large meeting in the square in mid-September 1891 from a window in the Listowel Arms Hotel. Less than three weeks later, on 6 October, Parnell died in Brighton, following a divorce scandal with Katharine O'Shea.

At Gunsborough, four miles north-west of Listowel, Horatio Herbert Kitchener, later to gain distinction as Earl Kitchener of Khartoum, was born on 15 June 1850. Close to the house of the Gun Mahony family is Kilmorna House, where Sir Arthur Vicars lived for the last years of his life. Vicars, as Ulster King of Arms, had been responsible for the safe-keeping of the Irish Crown Jewels in Dublin Castle. He fell under suspicion when the jewels were stolen in 1907. They were never recovered. Vicars, who co-operated with the British forces in Listowel, was shot dead outside his house as a spy by the IRA.

A distinguished Listowel family were the O'Rahillys, relations of the 1916 leader, The O'Rahilly. Alfred, Thomas and Cecile O'Rahilly were academics and professors. Alfred, a professor of mathematical physics, became President of

University College Cork and following his wife's death he joined the priesthood. Cecile and Thomas were professors of Celtic Studies and Thomas was also author of *Early Irish History and Mythology*.

By 1916 a branch of the Irish Volunteers had been established in the Listowel area. Ernest Blythe became a full-time organiser for the Kerry region. On 17 June 1920 the RIC constables in Listowel Barracks were ordered to hand over the barracks to British troops, and to transfer to different stations. Constable Jeremiah Mee was the first to refuse the order on 19 June. In total fourteen constables resigned, in what became known as the Mutiny of Listowel Barracks. District Inspector O'Sullivan was targeted by the IRA and on 19 January 1921 he was assassinated. The gunmen from Moyvane made good their escape and two Listowel men were arrested for the murder. The town also featured in the Civil War and in August 1922 240 troops who had crossed the Shannon from Kilrush and landed at Tarbert took Listowel and later all of north Kerry.

Listowel has long been regarded as the literary capital of Kerry, being the birthplace and home of many prominent writers. George Fitzmaurice, born on 28 January 1877 in Bedford House near Listowel, became well-known as an Abbey Theatre playwright, with such plays as *The Country Dressmaker*, *The Magic Glasses* and *The Dandy Dolls* to his credit. Maurice Walsh the novelist

LISTOWEL

was born on 2 May 1879, at Ballydonoghue near Listowel, and wrote such books as *The Key Above the Door*, *Blackcock's Feather* and *The Quiet Man*, which was filmed by John Ford in 1951. Bryan MacMahon, born on 29 September 1909, was a school teacher who first came to prominence as a writer with his contributions to the magazine, *The Bell*. His wide range of novels, plays and short stories include *Song of Anvil*, *The Bugle in the Blood*, *The Honey Spike*, *Children of the Rainbow* and *The Master*. The playwright, novelist and publican John B. Keane was born here on 21 July 1928. His many successful plays include *Sive*, *The Field* and *Big Maggie* and his books include *The Bodhrán Maker* and *Durango*. The town is also the birthplace of the historian Fr J. Anthony Gaughan, who produced such works as *Listowel and its Vicinity*, *Thomas Johnson* and *Alfred O'Rahilly*. Two other well-known local characters are Mick and the late Sean McCarthy, the latter the writer of such evergreen ballads as *Step it Out Mary* and *Shanagolden*. In recent years, Mick, who was the former proprietor of the Embankment pub in Tallaght, has written his autobiography.

Every May the town plays host to Writers' Week, a major event on the literary calendar when writers from home and abroad converge on the market town to attend workshops, plays, recite poetry and discuss writing. Other important events associated with Listowel are the Fleadh Cheoil na hÉireann, the national festival of traditional music, and the Listowel Races, which began in 1858.

The old graveyard near Listowel where famine victims are buried. This shrine (right) is the only memorial in a field with no headstones, where many visitors of Irish descent lay wreaths and pay their respects to their ancestors who died in the Great Irish Famine. Below: a simple sign marks the entrance.

Moyvane

Moyvane is a small village situated seven miles north of Listowel. It comprises the two old parishes of Knockanure and Murher. Originally it was part of the territory of O'Connor Kerry, who resided at Carrigafoyle Castle, near Ballylongford. They built other castles in the area, at Ahalanna, on the banks of the Leitrim River and at Glenalappa, north-west of the village. In 1666 the Provost of Trinity College acquired all the lands in the vicinity and retained them until the beginning of this century.

To the traveller the village may seem off the beaten track but it is worth the short journey from Listowel to experience its tranquillity. To me it is a place where time seems to stand still. Those fortunate enough might experience a poetry reading by local teacher/poet, Gabriel Fitzmaurice. Con Brosnan, winner of six All-Ireland football medals, was also from here. The father of the poet Thomas Moore was born in the village. Moyvane (Máigh Mheáin: The Middle Plain; Murher is Máigh Oirthir, the Eastern Plain), was once called Newtown Sandes after the Cromwellian landlords named Sandes. The parish was run by the Augustinians of Rattoo, from the fourteenth century. The Dominican friars established a small community here around 1740. In 1841 the population of the village was 314 but by 1966 it had scarcely changed, at 294. The population of the entire parish stood at 3,293 in 1841 but had dropped to 1,456 in 1966.

Most priests were neutral towards the Whiteboys who were active in the district. These were a secret society which emerged among the peasantry in the west of Ireland around 1711, and again in 1761. The Whiteboys, who wore white smocks to conceal their identity, waged war against landlords and tithe-proctors and even against the priests when they charged exorbitant fees. They would rob and burn houses, kill cattle and burn corn and hay collected

RECOMMENDED

Knockanure monument (south of the village) to those who died there in May 1921.

Kearney's Bar, traditional music.

in tithe barns. On 4 May 1824 Fr Michael O'Sullivan called his parishioners into the chapel and passed three resolutions. The first expressed their abhorrence against recent outrages committed in Murher and the surrounding district. Secondly, they indicated their willingness to donate £26 to anyone giving information for burning houses in the parish and thirdly they recorded their thanks to Fr O'Sullivan. Samuel Lewis recorded in 1837 that Moyvane had a small thatched chapel with a school attached.

On October 25 1886 a meeting of the Irish National League was held in the village. It was addressed by John Dillon MP, Timothy Harrington MP and Fr Casey PP of Abbeyfeale. A resolution was passed that the name of Newtown Sandes 'be changed henceforth to Newtown Dillon'. Eventually the name reverted to Newtown Sandes. During the 1880s the landlord George Sandes was so despised that locals made a determined effort to change the name. In 1916 Dr Timothy Wolfe, a local doctor, had the village renamed Newtown Clarke after the executed 1916 leader, Tom Clarke. This naturally led to confusion as most people referred to it as Newtown Sandes. It was not until 1939 that Fr O'Sullivan, the parish priest, made a successful attempt to rename the village Moyvane.

On 5 June 1920 the RIC barracks, which had been vacated, was burned down by the IRA. Close to Moyvane is Knockanure (Cnoc an Dubhair, the Hill of the yew tree) where a tragic incident occurred on 12 May 1921. That day four colleagues, Jerry Lyons, Patrick Dalton, Con Dee and Patrick Walsh, sat chatting on Gortaglanna Bridge when a Black and Tan patrol arrived. The men were taken captive, questioned and lined up. Then the Tans coldbloodedly opened fire on them and Lyons, Dalton and Walsh were shot dead. Dee made good his escape. Their bodies were dragged behind the Tan lorries. The ballad *The Valley of Knockanure* was fashioned by Bryan MacMahon from material supplied by Pádraig Ó Ceallacháin (a national school teacher at Knockanure) and gives an account of the incident.

You may sing and speak of Easter week,
And the heroes of ninety-eight,
Of the Fenian men who roamed the glens,
In victory or defeat.
Their names on history's pages are told,
Their memory will endure.
Not a song was sung of our darling sons
In the valley of Knockanure.

Left: in the new church at Knockanure, a wooden panel sculpted by Oisín Kelly depicts the twelve apostles. Right: stations of the cross in applique tapestry by Leslie McWeeney.

Ballyduff

Ballyduff can be reached by turning left on the Listowel to Ballybunion road at Lisselton. The original village was situated on a hill. In the early 1820s when word came through that the British army was approaching to recruit or force men to join the force every man, woman and child vacated the village. The British were so incensed to find it deserted that they burned it to the ground. Soon after, a new village in its present position was constructed with the name Ballyduff, An Baile Dubh (the black or dark town).

This is another small village with a wide main street. Recently the local branch of Comhaltas Ceoltóirí Éireann was revived and they plan to stage regular musical evenings. Another energetic group is the Ballyduff Drama Group which stages several productions each year. Drive south through the village, and a short distance on take a left turn following a signpost. This will bring you to Rattoo Round Tower (the parish name is Rath Tuaig, meaning north fort). The ninety-two foot tower was built over a thousand years ago. Legend has it that when the monks vacated the tower, rather than leave the bell for the plundering troops they threw it into the river. It is reputed that the bell rang out calling the monks back. The tower was associated with an early Celtic church which was removed stone by stone and rebuilt in Ballybunion. I would also recommend a visit to Rattoo Heritage Museum, which has exhibits relevant to the North Kerry area from all periods of history.

The first church of Rattoo was founded by Bishop Lughdach of Uí Fearba and was granted to Meyler Fitzhenry in 1200. It was the Church of St Peter and St Paul, founded for Knights Hospitallers and later given to the Canons Regular of Saint Augustine. Nearby was the hospital of John the Baptist. At a local holy well lepers came in search of a cure. In 1600 the harper Michael Dall was to submit to the authorities and give sureties to keep the peace. That same year the abbey was burned by the Irish when Sir Charles Wilmot took possession of the area. The ruins of the church are in the ancient burial ground.

On the road into Ballyduff is the Cashen River. Close to the mouth of the river, at Ballyeagh, a vicious 'Faction Fight' took place in 1834. The Cooleens fought the Black Mulvihills, leaving sixteen people either killed in the fighting or drowned. In the early 1850s the first timber bridge was built over the Cashen River. Prior to that, the river had to be forded. Early this century the first iron bridge was erected and in 1960 the present bridge was built.

In 1920 the Stoughtons' big house at nearby Ballyhorgan was destroyed by the IRA. One incident during the Civil War will never be forgotten locally. In April 1923 Timothy (Aeroplane) Lyons and five Republican companions went on the run from Free State troops and sought shelter in Clashmealcon Caves, north of Kerry Head. From the cliff above, the 'Free Staters' tried unsuccessfully to burn them out with blazing bales of hay. Two of the men, Patrick O'Shea and Tony McGrath, drowned while trying to escape and seek help. Reinforcements armed with machine-guns and grenades came from Tralee and launched a bombardment on the caves. Finally Lyons agreed to surrender and after much discussion a rope was lowered to him. As he climbed up, it either broke or was cut and he fell to his death. His body lying on the rocks was riddled with bullets. Following the three-day siege the other men surrendered. Three of them were later executed in Tralee.

... WITH BRIGHTLY COLOURED BUILDINGS ...

Causeway

The village of Causeway is four miles west of Ballyduff, on the road to Ballyheigue, in the townland of Dromkeen West. The parish has a long rugged coastline with cliffs. Causeway derives its name from its location at the northern side of an old passageway which once crossed the marsh and bogland — the Red Bog. The old Irish name, Tóchar, still survives at the southern end where there is the townland of Tocharbawn.

The name Causeway would appear to be of comparatively recent origin, the older name, Killury, having been used as far back as 1387. Prior to that date it had been known as Killuregy. In diocesan records the parish was known as Killury, and with Ballyheigue and Rattoo formed one administrative unit for church purposes. Several legends exist as to the origins of the name Killury, in Irish Cill Lúraigh. One tells of three sister saints in the locality named Lúraí, Maoile, and Athann who built three churches which were appropriately named Cill Lúraigh, Cill Maoile and Cill Athann (Killury, Kilmoyley and Killahan).

The village, with brightly coloured buildings, is neatly situated at a crossroads. Harty's seafood restaurant is heartily recommended for a good meal. A suitable venue for a relaxing drink is Keane's pub. Another important feature of the village is the comprehensive school, opened in 1982, which draws pupils from a wide catchment area.

In the mid-eighteenth century John Nelan, a wine merchant, built Sandford House, on the eastern outskirts of the village. An imposing three-storey building, in 1782 it became the residence of his son Fr Nicholas Nelan, parish priest. The house had gun turrets and a force of yeomanry who gave Fr Nelan protection in his capacity as Justice of the Peace. The Protestant church was built in the late 1780s and tithes were collected to support the clergy.

For many centuries villagers collected seaweed with pikes at low tide and because of the rocky nature of the shoreline had to transfer it on their backs in 'cliabhs' or pannier baskets to carts nearby. The seaweed was used to fertilise the fields. There was a fair field in the village where six cattle fairs were held annually up to 1959. Blacksmiths in the village were exceptionally busy for some days before horse fairs in Listowel and Tralee.

Meenoghane, north of the village, was a noted centre for smuggling and many illicit cargoes of silk and spirits were landed there. In 1915, following the sinking of the *Lusitania* by the Germans, the bodies of three victims of the tragedy were washed ashore there.

In 1977 a survey indicated that Causeway contained ninety-three buildings including the old presbytery and barracks, a dance hall and dispensary. There was a population of 273 people.

RECOMMENDED

Harty's Seafood Restaurant.
Keane's pub.

... ANCIENT SEAT OF THE EARLS OF KERRY ...

Lixnaw

The small village of Lixnaw, on the River Brick, is situated about five miles from Listowel. The name, Leic Snámha, means that it was a safe place to swim across the ford. In early times it had several names including Kilcaragh, Beillic and Tuberhine. It was also known as Lisanaw. The village was once in the parish of Kilcarraigh, in the barony of Clanmaurice. Lixnaw has several impressive buildings including the Railway Bar, Presentation Convent and the adjoining St Michael's Catholic Church which recently had a new spire added. The local branch of Comhaltas Ceoltóirí Éireann hold regular musical evenings.

A castle built there in the thirteenth century was the main seat of the Fitzmaurices, Knights of Kerry and Lixnaw. Nicholas, the third Baron Lixnaw, made many improvements in the village including the building of a bridge in 1320. On 26 July 1568 a bloody battle was fought there between the forces of Thomas Fitzmaurice and James Fitzmaurice Fitzgerald, a relative of the Earl of Desmond and Conor O'Connor Kerry. It was to become known as the Battle of Lixnaw, and O'Connor Kerry was killed. In the early 1600s the castle changed hands on a number of occasions. When the Elizabethan commander Sir Charles Wilmot attacked the castle in 1602, the Irishmen inside the castle decided to burn and abandon it. Lord Kerry succeeded in recapturing it in 1610 and entrusted its defence to his brother, Gerald, but he was forced to surrender the castle back to Wilmot when his force ran out of water. Around 1680 the Knights of Kerry built a family residence there and lived there until the mid 1760s. East of Lixnaw is a monument to John, third Knight of Kerry.

The travel writer Arthur Young commented in 1776: 'Called in to view Lixnaw, the ancient seat of the Earls of Kerry, but deserted for ten years past, and now presents so melancholy a scene of desolation, that it shocked me to see it. Everything around lies in ruins, and the house itself is going fast by thieving depredations of the neighbourhood.'

The Catholic district of Lixnaw comprised the parishes of Kilcarraigh and Kiltoomy and portions of Dysert, Finuge and Kilfeighny, and contained the chapels of Lixnaw, built in 1805, and Iveamore. Superior quality limestone was found in the vicinity and was used for building and ornamental purposes. Boats brought sand and seaweed, which was used to fertilise the land, up the River Cashen and from there up the River Brick to the village.

In 1837 Samuel Lewis gave an assessment of Lixnaw: 'It consists of two streets of tolerably good houses, and contains a spacious RC chapel, and a school supported by subscription, to which Mrs Raymond contributes £6 per annum. A court for the manor of Lixnaw is held every three weeks, on Monday, for the recovery of debts not exceeding forty shillings late currency. A patent exists for four fairs, but they are not at present held.'

The Presentation Order founded a convent in the village in 1877. A Land League meeting was held in Lixnaw on 25 September 1881 to press for the improvement of labourers' conditions. Eight thousand people attended a meeting which had Moore Stack (father of Austin Stack who was leader of the Kerry volunteers and first Minister for Home Affairs) among the platform party. Stack and some others founded the first GAA club in the county. In June 1923 the barracks was burned.

RECOMMENDED

Four miles north-east on the Listowel road is the folk theatre at Finuge with traditional music during the summer.

Lixnaw Agricultural Museum (June-Sept).

St Michael's Catholic Church.

Presentation Convent.

Quilters Bar, traditional music.

... MANY HOUSES FRESHLY WHITEWASHED ...

Abbeydorney

Abbeydorney is a small village, seven miles north of Tralee, on the road between Lixnaw and Ardfert. From Ardfert, take the road east to the village, which centres around a crossroads with two large pubs situated on two of the corners. Many houses have been freshly whitewashed and an unusual flat-roofed derelict house with purple windows and door is prominent in the main street. O'Donovan's shop in the village offers a wide range of goods as it is a hardware store, a butcher's and a post office and has an interesting window display of boots and old tools. St Bernard's Catholic church is set out in tiers in an unorthodox design. The station has been renovated but the old signal box is in bad repair. Across the fields behind the station is the Cistercian Abbey.

The original village was in the parish of O'Dorney, in the union of Listowel and the barony of Clanmaurice. North of the village the Cistercian Abbey or Kyrie Eleison at O'Dorney or Mainistir Ó dTórna was established in 1154 by the monks from Mellifont Abbey. According to the Annals of the Four Masters, the village took its name from this ancient Abbey of Kyrie Eleison or O'Dorney. The first Abbot of Mellifont, Gilla Chríost Ó Conairche, later to become Bishop of Lismore and Papal Legate, died there in 1186. The Abbot was also a lord in Parliament but seldom sat in the House. The tuatha (chief) of a local tribe, the Uí dTorna, were also based there.

Samuel Lewis's *Topographical Dictionary of Ireland* of 1837 described Abbeydorney thus: 'The village consists mostly of thatched houses, a constabulary police station; and a manorial court is held occasionally. The Roman Catholic parochial chapel, built here in 1826, at the expense of £600,

is a spacious edifice fronted with a stone, in the later English style, and embellished with a fine altar-piece and painting. Near the village is a flour-mill.'

Mr and Mrs Hall in their travel book, *Hall's Ireland,* written in 1840 stated: 'In the village of O'Dorney are the ruins of another abbey — a shapeless pile — but the deformity of which is hidden by the ivy that covers the whole of it.'

A company of the Irish Volunteers was formed in Abbeydorney, known as the O'Dorney Volunteers. On 22 November 1914 Austin Stack, commandant of the Tralee Volunteers, addressed a large rally in the village. On Good Friday 1916 Sergeant Daniel Bailey, a former member of the Royal Irish Rifles, landed with Sir Roger Casement at Banna Strand. Bailey and Robert Monteith walked into Tralee to seek assistance from Austin Stack. Bailey was arrested and taken to Abbeydorney police-barracks where under questioning he revealed the whereabouts of his comrades and the planned landing of arms at Fenit. Austin Stack spoke at many public meetings including one at Abbeydorney on 31 July 1917 at which he advocated that the crowd should join Sinn Féin. The following month he was arrested for inciting disaffection among the civilian population, and sentenced to two years' imprisonment.

The Abbeydorney railway branch line from Tralee closed on 2 June 1978.

In 1986 the village was a focal point for the famous 'Kerry Babies' Inquiry following the discovery of a baby's body on White Strand, Cahirciveen, and another in a local field.

RECOMMENDED

Cistercian Abbey, north of village.

St Bernard's Catholic church.

Old Railway Station.

... A VILLAGE NEARBY BANNA STRAND ...

Ballyheigue

Ballyheigue is a coastal village and its sandy beach stretches eight miles into Tralee Bay. In 1312 Ballyheigue (Ballytayg), Baile Uí Thaidhg, Town of Tadhg (referring to Tadhg Cantillon, see below), was the centre of the Febra O'Laoghain. There was once a total of twenty-four townlands in the parish: Ballyheigue, Ballylongane, Ballyronan, Bouleenshere, Ballinclemissig, Buncurrig, Caherulla, Castleshannon, Cloghane-bawn, Clahaneleesh, Dirtaine, Doonmountain, Dreenagh, Dromature, Dromgower, Glendahalin, Glenlea, Glenderry, Heirhill, Knockane, Maulin, Tiduff, Tiershanahan and Tonereigh.

This is another tourist resort which caters for family holidays with several hotels, guest houses and caravan parks. I favour it over Ballybunion as it is less congested and commercialised. There are sand-dunes and an impressive safe sandy beach which extends eight miles into Tralee Bay. There is a fair-size car park beside the beach. Ballyheigue Pattern day is still held annually in September. The traveller should visit Ballyheigue Castle and the Roger Casement monument overlooking the beach.

In Ballyheigue Bay is an area known as 'Teampall-fóthoinn', the Church under the Waves, which according to legend was once a burial ground, covered by sea and still submerged. 'The Bullauns' is an area on the rocks where coffins of those to be buried at sea were placed. Beneath Trisk Mountain are the ruins of St Macadaw's church and well.

In Norman times the Cantillons, originally de Cantlupe, a Catholic family, held Ballyheigue and Tadhg de Cantillon built the first Ballyheigue Castle, with a thatched roof. The lands were confiscated from the Cantillons and given to a Protestant planter named Crosbie by Queen Elizabeth I. This was part of her plan to prosecute the Catholic church and replace it with a Protestant one. In 1585 Thomas Cantillon built Ballingarry Castle for the Earl of Desmond. Later it was held by Red Garret Stack who surrendered it to Colonel David Crosbie in 1602. Crosbie rebuilt the castle in 1641, adding a drawbridge.

William Morrison designed the present Ballyheigue Castle, a neo-gothic building, for the Crosbie family and it was constructed in 1710. The tower was added in 1812. On 28 October 1730 a Danish ship, *The Golden Lyon*, was led onto rocks in Ballyheigue Bay by a false signal set up by the Crosbies. The ship was carrying a cargo of silver, iron and other valuables. The crew was rescued

BALLYHEIGUE CASTLE

by Sir Thomas Crosbie, MP for Kerry, and the valuables were stored in the castle for safekeeping. Sir Thomas died suddenly but other members of his family decided to steal the silver and launched an attack on the castle. They found the chests empty as the valuables had been hidden in caves beneath the castle. There was speculation that Lady Margaret Crosbie was behind the action.

A curious feature of Ballyheigue is that there is no Catholic church in the village itself. This is because the Crosbies would not allow any building in the village to be taller than their own residence and the Catholic church had to be constructed some distance outside the village on land donated by a farmer. Close to the church is Our Lady's Holy Well where Mass was said during Penal days. Adjoining the well is a grotto to the Blessed Virgin, patron of the parish. Another Holy Well, St Brigid's Well is at Glendahalin on Kerry Head. Legend has it that St Brigid frequently visited the convent there.

Also on Kerry Head is Kilvicada (Church of the son of Deaghadh), an ancient church dating to St Erc's time, the fifth century. Two round stones blessed by the saint are believed to have had curing powers. Kerry Head is noted for 'Kerry Diamonds', perfectly formed quartz crystals, with six-sided conical ends, peculiar to the Kerry Mountains.

In 1921 the British authorities used Ballyheigue Castle as a prison and troops rounded up local men suspected of being in the IRA and incarcerated them there. Mrs Erskine, owner of the castle, decided to sell the furniture and the IRA waited until after the auction before destroying the building on 27 May 1921. On 30 October 1922 a detachment of Free State troops surrounded Ballyheigue and John Lawlor, a young local Republican who tried to evade them was shot dead.

The disabled writer Christy Brown, author of *My Left Foot*, lived with his wife, Mary, in the area for a number of years in the 1970s. A statue of Roger Casement has been erected overlooking Ballyheigue Bay in memory of his fateful landing on nearby Banna Strand.

RECOMMENDED

Ballyheigue Castle.
The beach and sand-dunes.
Roger Casement Monument.
Kerry Head, ideal for viewing Dingle peninsula and also for fishing.
O'Regan's Bar, traditional music.
Gigi Restaurant and Grill, run by Luis Garcia

... BRENDAN THE NAVIGATOR'S MONASTERY ...

Ardfert

The village of Ardfert is five miles north-west of Tralee on the Ballyheigue Road. Its name in Irish is Ard–Fhearta (the Height of the Grave). The village has also been known as Ard Art and Ard Erc. In 461 one of St Patrick's companions, Bishop Erc, was appointed to Ardfert. Later he was to baptise St Brendan, who was born in 484 AD. Bishop Erc went on to educate and ordain Brendan, when the saint was thirty. Brendan later distinguished himself as Brendan the Navigator and became patron saint of Kerry. Legend has it that a drawing of the monastery was snatched from Brendan's hand by a crow and the parchment dropped on a hillock at Ardfert. St Brendan established a monastery there and later a cathedral with the aid of his monks. After Brendan's death in 577 the area also became known as Ardfert-Bhreandáin.

Ardfert can be best reached by taking the main road north from Fenit. It is a small town which would attract little attention but for its ecclesiastical heritage. The traveller should allow a reasonable amount of time to explore the historic sites of the area. The dominant features are St Brendan's Cathedral and the Franciscan Friary. *Ardfert Past and Present* is a helpful book on history and folklore produced by the Ardfert Youth Club and available locally.

In 1046 lightning destroyed the stone church which was later restored. In 1111 it was destroyed again by O'Cuilein, a local warring faction. Amchad Ó hAnmah, the Bishop of Ardfert, died in 1117. At the Synod of Kells in 1152 Ardfert became the See for Kerry. In 1180 the cathedral was burned again and Bishop O'Conarchy began to build a new church, Teampall na hÓighe, Church of the Virgin, which was completed a decade later. Building of the new cathedral commenced in 1199 and it was ready for worship sixteen years later. In 1253 Thomas Fitzmaurice, first Lord of Kerry, founded a Franciscan friary east of the cathedral. It was called Ardfert Abbey and dedicated to St Brendan.

The Annals of the Four Masters credited the McCarthy family with building the friary in the following entry in 1340: 'The Monastery of Oirbhealach, at Carraig-an-Chiuil, at the eastern end of Loch Lein, in the diocese of Ardfert, in Munster, was founded for Franciscan friars by McCarthy More, prince of Desmond (Donnell, son of Teige), and the chiefs of the country selected burial for themselves in this monastery. Among these were O'Sullivan More and the two O'Donohues.'

The monks were expelled in 1540 and the building was later used to house Elizabethan soldiers. The second Lord Kerry built a leper house nearby. In the fifteenth century a small late Romanesque Church, Teampall na Griffin, was erected north-west of the cathedral. Ardfert was a bishop's see, held in common with the bishopric of Limerick until 1661.

In the early 1600s Ardfert became a borough and for a time returned two members to the Irish Parliament. The Fitzmaurices were Lords of Kerry from the thirteenth to seventeenth centuries and after their demise the Crosbies became the dominant family in the area. David Crosbie, who fought against the rebels in 1641, was appointed Governor of Kerry by Oliver Cromwell. During the rising the insurgents attacked and burned Lord Kerry's castle to the ground. Sparks from the blaze blew onto the thatched roof of the nearby cathedral, starting a fire that reduced it to a shell. Tradition has it that at one

time Ardfert had seven churches. A round tower, 120 feet high, used as a belfry and place of refuge by the monks, was built chiefly of dark marble. It stood near the west front of the cathedral, but collapsed in a storm in 1771. Faction fights regularly broke out in the village between local feuding families.

In 1796 in *A Frenchman's Walk Through Ireland*, De Latocnaye recorded; 'I went on Sunday to the Catholic chapel. The women are always separated from the men here. I suppose this is to avoid distraction. In the middle of the service the priest made a long discourse in Irish, afterwards translating the principal part into English. He consigned to all the devils (although in highly proper terms) all those infamous enough not to pay their dues.'

Sir Maurice Crosbie, first Viscount Crosbie, built a distinctive Georgian house with a bowling green. It was through the influence of the Crosbies that Ardfert became the first village in North Kerry to have piped running water in most houses. In the main the Crosbies were benevolent landlords but the most notorious member of the family was William Talbot Crosbie, known as 'Billy the Leveller' because he razed the houses of insurgents to the ground in the late nineteenth century. The Crosbie residence was burned down in May 1921.

A parade of the Tralee and Ardfert Volunteers took place on 28 June 1914

and was inspected by Pádraig Pearse. On Good Friday 21 April 1916 Sir Roger Casement, the Irish patriot, landed on Banna Strand, close to Ardfert, from a submarine, U-19, which had accompanied the *Aud* on her ill-fated journey from Germany with arms for the IRB. Casement, who was ill, hid in McKenna's Fort while his colleagues went to Tralee to seek the assistance of Austin Stack. McKenna's Fort is situated in a field by the roadside, west of Ardfert. He was arrested by the Ardfert police before the return of his colleagues who were later also arrested. He was held overnight in Ardfert barracks and the next day was taken in a pony and cart to Tralee. Casement was tried in London, convicted and hanged for treason on 3 August 1916. On 28 July 1968 a monument was erected on Banna Strand to commemorate Casement's landing.

RECOMMENDED

St Brendan's Cathedral.

Franciscan Friary.

McKenna's Fort, 1 mile north of the village, a monument to Roger Casement.

O'Sullivan's Cottage Bar, traditional music.

Fenit

The small village of Fenit (Fhianait, the Wild Place), eight miles from Tralee, is arguably the most important port in County Kerry. It has long been regarded as being the harbour of Tralee, as large vessels which could not reach Blennerville could discharge there in safety. A lifeboat station was built in 1879 to serve Tralee Bay. The first sail lifeboat was manned by ten oarsmen. Seven boats served at the station. The pier is an impressive structure from which there are marvellous views of the Dingle peninsula. It is a recommended area for angling, swimming and sailboarding. Occasionally fish can be bought directly from the fishing boats as they return with their catch.

In 1880 an Act of Parliament set up an administrative body — Tralee and Fenit Pier and Harbour Commissioners — to develop the port and build a pier and a viaduct to connect Samphire Island to the mainland. The pier extends 1,700 feet from the mainland. The Rowan family were collectors of taxes for the port of Tralee around 1850. A customs house was built in Fenit in 1910 to facilitate the importation and exportation of goods through Fenit Pier. Agricultural produce from the surrounding districts was the prime export.

By the beginning of the 1800s the village consisted of small fishermen's cottages around the seashore. During the mackerel season, boats from as far as the Isle of Man, Scotland and France would converge on the port to fish the lucrative Atlantic. A regular oyster fleet operating out of the port dredged the oyster beds. During the Fenit Regatta there was an oyster boat race. When big ships were approaching the port there was a race amongst the pilots to reach them first and whichever pilot got there first escorted the ship into Fenit Pier.

The Tralee and Fenit Railway was authorised in 1880 to build an eight-mile branch line from Tralee to the deep-water port for the transportation of fish to the market. The line opened on 5 July 1887 and was operated by the Waterford and Limerick Railway. In the summer months passengers from Tralee travelled out to Fenit beach. The line was not profitable and the company went bankrupt, but the Waterford, Limerick and Western Railway continued to operate it until 1920 when that company was taken over by the Great Southern and Western Railway who operated it until its closure in 1960.

Fenit Castle was built on a limestone rock at the north-eastern extremity of Fenit Island to defend the entrance to Barrow Harbour, which once had a reasonable trade with Spain and the Low Countries. This was a Fitzmaurice castle. Northwards is Barrow Harbour, close to which is Church Hill, the parish church of Ballynahaglish. The Round Castle of Barrow was built in the thirteenth century. There is disagreement among historians as to whether the Fitzmaurices or the de Clahulls were the original owners of the castle. The three-ringed Rath of Barrow is reputed to be a home of Aenach na mBerrain, King of Cashel. Nearby is an ancient burial ground.

Charles Smith wrote in *The Ancient and Present State of the County of Kerry* (1756): 'More to the south is Fennit Island, part of the Earl of Kerry's estate on which is an old castle, built to defend the entrance of a small creek, where vessels with the assistance of a pilot, may enter in bad weather. Towards the north point of Fennit, are several sunk rocks, and also one above the water called the Rose'.

It is widely believed that Brendan the Navigator was born near Fenit in 484.

Spa, four miles from Fenit, is so named because it was popular for its waters and mineral spring in the eighteenth century.

In September 1915 Austin Stack and other Kerry leaders decided that Fenit would be the most appropriate place on the coast for the landing of arms from Germany. By the following spring the Kerry Volunteers were well trained but were in need of arms for their participation in the Easter Rising. Plans were set in motion to land arms in Fenit on Easter Sunday 1916. The Tralee Volunteers were to take Fenit Pier, unload the arms and distribute them throughout Cork and Limerick. On Holy Thursday the German ship, the *Aud*, sailed in close looking for a signal which was not given. The following day Sir Roger Casement landed on Banna Strand from a submarine which accompanied the *Aud*. As he was ill, he hid close to Ardfert while his companions travelled to Tralee to seek help. Casement was discovered and arrested by Ardfert police. He was ent to London for trial, and hanged for treason in August 1916.

On 2 August 1922, 450 Free State troops from Limerick made a surprise landing at Fenit on board the *Lady Wicklow* under Brigadier Patrick O'Leary. On hearing that Free State troops were marching on Tralee the Republicans burned Ballymullen barracks but the town was quickly captured.

In February 1941 the German spy, Herman Goertz, attempted to escape by trawler from Fenit but the police were alerted and the plan aborted.

RECOMMENDED

Tralee Sailing Club.
Tralee eighteen hole golf course at Barrow.
Ring fort above the village.
Barrow Strand.

Tralee

The pale moon was rising above the green mountain,
The sun was declining beneath the blue sea;
When I strayed with my love to the pure crystal fountain,
That stands in the beautiful vale of Tralee.
She was lovely and fair as the rose of the summer,
Yet 'twas not her beauty alone that won me,
Oh no! 'Twas the truth in her eye ever dawning
That made me love Mary, the Rose of Tralee.

This evergreen song about Mary O'Connor, the original Rose of Tralee, was written by William Pembroke Mulchinock in 1845. Mulchinock, a member of a wealthy Tralee family, was in love with Mary who worked as a maid in his uncle's house. Shortly afterwards Mary died and a shattered Mulchinock emigrated to America. In 1953 a memorial was erected to her in Tralee town park. The song has been immortalised by many singers including John McCormack. The town has become famous for its annual 'Rose of Tralee' festival when Roses of Irish descent from all over the world gather for the occasion.

This is a bustling town with a good range of shops, arcades, quality restaurants and a lively night life. Siamsa presents regular shows during the summer season. The town has a hospital, court house, a newspaper — *The Kerryman* — and several hotels. Not the ideal spot for those seeking a peaceful holiday, the town centre regularly suffers from traffic congestion and it is often difficult to find a parking space. The library has an excellent local history section for those interested in the heritage or folklore of the area. There is a large park in the town centre, suitable for picnics. An important recent development was the commencement of work on the Tralee-Blennerville steam railway. A trip on this line will bring the traveller to Blennerville windmill, museum and craft centre.

Tralee (Tráigh Lí) or Trá Lí, which takes its name from the River Lee which flows into Tralee Bay, is the main town and administrative centre for the county. A Geraldine castle was built there in 1230 by John FitzThomas Fitzgerald, ancestor of the Earls of Desmond, on the banks of the river and was manned by a constable and garrison. The Earl of Desmond established his seat in the castle and administered North Kerry and West Limerick from there. He annually presided over a gathering of the freeholders of the county in the castle. The men had to supply food and the women had to prepare it, and any woman failing to turn up was fined twenty shillings.

In 1243 the Priory of Holy Cross was founded west of the castle by John, son of Thomas Fitzgerald, Prince of Desmond, for the Dominican friars. The Priory was to play an important part in establishing Tralee as small vessels could sail up to its walls with favourable tides. The Priory was extensively reconstructed in the fifteenth century and enjoyed the patronage of the Desmonds for several centuries. Many members of the family were buried within its grounds. The first occupants of its tombs were Thomas Fitzgerald and his son Maurice, who were both slain at Callan in 1261 in a fight with the McCarthy Mór. The Town Hall and Gate House were constructed in 1286.

The Norman knight John FitzThomas Fitzgerald, a descendant of the Welsh princess Nesta, established a colony at Tralee because of its strategic importance, being a junction of routes in the old Kingdom of Kerry, with direct access to the sea. In the following century FitzThomas and his descendants, the powerful Earls of Desmond, used Tralee as a stronghold to develop the strongest Anglo-Norman seat in Munster. The Fitzgeralds favoured the Irish cause in preference to the English and the family was well liked by the locals. The town grew up on the northern side of the salt marshes and succeeded in attracting farmers, craftsmen and merchants from England. A charter was issued which entitled new arrivals to hold annual fairs and a weekly market. The town developed quickly as a market town and port, with dealers selling their goods in the open. The settlers built houses and streets which stretched northwards.

In 1579 Henry Davells, one of the Commissioners for Munster, came to the castle to seek the assistance of the Earl of Desmond against the Spaniards who had landed at Smerwick Harbour, but he and the Provost-Marshal

Carter and their entourage were put to death by the Earl's brother, Sir John, the godson of the Davells. In 1580 Ormonde and Pelham gathered their forces and declared that they would clear every Spaniard from the district. As English forces marched on Tralee, Desmond set fire to the town. In 1583 the fifteenth and last Earl of Desmond, an elderly man, was killed by a soldier named Daniel O'Kelly. His head was despatched to London and Queen Elizabeth I ordered that it be impaled on a spike on London Bridge.

In September 1587 the castle and six thousand acres of Desmond lands were granted to Sir Edward Denny for his part in the massacre of the Spaniards at Smerwick Harbour. In 1613 the town became a borough and returned two members to the Irish Parliament until 1800 and then returned one until 1804 when it lost its borough status. The Dennys were associated with the town for over two centuries. They rebuilt the castle in 1620 but Sir Piaras Ferriter besieged it in 1641 and it was again destroyed. Two years later it fell to Murrough the Burner O'Brien. Lord Inchiquin came to Tralee to find it burned to the ground and in 1691 the Jacobite forces again burned it as the Williamite forces approached. Tralee was the seat of Bishop Mudgett from 1753-74. His successor, Bishop Moylan, encouraged by Lord Kenmare, resided in Killarney.

In 1762 a duel was fought between James Mahony and John Blennerhassett in a large room in the market house. Blennerhassett was killed and Mahony was charged with murder. In September 1798 Daniel O'Connell made his first court appearance here as a young barrister. Following his release from jail O'Connell visited Tralee. The townspeople paraded him through the streets and he addressed a large meeting in Denny Street.

By the middle of the nineteenth century Tralee had been well established as a market town and most of the inhabitants made their living from the land or in the trades. Development was accelerated with the introduction of the railway. The first line, from Mallow to Tralee, was built by the Killarney Junction Railway in 1859. In 1883 the line was extended to Limerick. Later branch lines were opened to Killorglin, Cahirciveen and Valentia Island. A narrow gauge line was extended to Dingle, running south-east to cross the ship canal at Blennerville and thence travelled along the coast below the Slieve Mish Mountains. The Court House in Ashe Street was designed by Sir Richard Morrison and also built in the nineteenth century.

A mile outside Tralee is Blennerville, originally called Tramore, Cathair-Modrain. The Blennerhassett family first came to County Kerry in 1586 during the Munster Plantation. One member of the family, Sir Rowland Blennerhassett settled in the area and developed it into a village calling it after himself. In 1760 John Blennerhassett, long time father (longest serving member) of the Irish House of Commons, built Ballyseedy Castle. In 1780 he built a flour mill and a windmill which became one of the most prominent landmarks in the village. The windmill is over sixty-eight feet high and is one of the largest traditional windmills. With the Repeal of the Corn Laws in 1848 and the importation of cheap corn from America the mill experienced great trading difficulties. The mill changed hands several times and operated until the 1880s, and the flour produced was exported to England and the Continent. In 1984 restoration work commenced on the windmill and it is now open to the public along with a visitor centre, craft shops and a coffee shop.

A ship canal was constructed and opened in 1846, allowing steamships to reach Tralee for the importation of coal and timber and the export of grain. A drawbridge was also constructed at this juncture. Following the famine the starving people of Tralee and paupers from the workhouses throughout Kerry were given free passage to America. They made their way to Blennerville Quay, where there was also a workhouse, and were rowed out to the 'coffin ships' (so called because of the thousands of people who died during the voyage to America). Other passengers paid a fare of about £3.

In Scotia's Glen about three miles south of Tralee is the grave of Queen Scotia, a legendary Pharaoh's daughter who was slain in a battle against the

Tuatha Dé Danann on Slieve Mish Mountain. A large flagstone marks her grave. The nearby Caherconree Mountain takes its name from Cathair Chon-Raoi, the fort called after Cú-Raoi Mac Daire. Legend informs us that Cú-Raoi's unfaithful wife turned the waters of the Finglas stream white with milk to inform her husband's enemies of his presence. They climbed the mountain, captured him and put him to death.

In 1842 William Makepeace Thackeray gave an account of Tralee in *The Irish Sketch Book*. 'There seems to be a good deal of poor business going on; the town thronged with people as usual; the shops large and not too splendid. There are two or three rows of respectable houses, and a mall, and the town's people have the further privilege of walking in the neighbouring grounds of a handsome park. Tralee has a newspaper, and boasts of a couple of clubs; the one I saw was a big white house, no windows broken, and looking comfortable.'

Tralee became an urban council in 1878. During the 1913-14 period many Volunteers were recruited in the area and Austin Stack became their leader. Stack was born in the Ballymullen area of Tralee, on 7 December 1879. He was jailed at various times for his political activities and went on hunger strike. He escaped from prison in England in October 1919 and was appointed Minister for Home Affairs in the second Dail in 1921. Pádraig Pearse visited Tralee late in 1914 and addressed five hundred Volunteers in the sportsfield. By 1919 there were two Kerry Brigades — one in Tralee for north and west Kerry, the other in Killarney for the west county. During the latter part of 1920 there were many outbreaks of violence in the district. In October two Black and Tans were thrown alive into a blazing pit. Later that month some RIC constables were shot and two were held hostage. The army kept the town under siege from 31 October for ten days. Many buildings, including the county building, were destroyed during this period. By December the entire county had been placed under martial law.

On 23 April 1922, in Tralee, Michael Collins declared that neither the Treaty nor the Republic were worth the risk of civil war. There was great bitterness in the Tralee area with the outbreak of civil war. On 2 August 1922 the Republicans who held Tralee were surprised by a force of 450 Free State troops who landed at Fenit and succeeded in taking the town. On 7 March 1923, in a reprisal for the killing of Lieutenant O'Connor and four Free State troops in Castleisland, Free State troops took nine Republican prisoners from Ballymullen barracks in Tralee, to clear a mine obstruction at Ballyseedy Cross,

RECOMMENDED

Kerry the Kingdom, Kerry County Museum, Ashe Memorial Hall (April to October).

Tralee-Blennerville Steam Railway (June - Oct).

Blennerville Windmill and Museum.

Siamsa Tíre, National Folk Theatre.

Rose of Tralee, end of August.

Tralee Races, end of August.

Tourist Office, Ashe Memorial Hall.

Bus Éireann Day Tours.

Dúchas, Edward Street, HQ Comhaltas Ceoltóirí Éireann, Kerry.

Greyhound Racing, Tuesday and Friday.

Horse drawn caravans for hire. Information at the Tourist Office.

Tralee Sports Complex and Swimming Pool.

Tralee Bowling Alley.

Waterworld (opening 1994)

three miles away. When they reached their destination the prisoners were tied together and the mine was detonated. Eight of the prisoners were killed and one man, Stephen Fuller, escaped. A monument to their memory, by the Breton sculptor Yann Renard-Goulet, was erected at the spot.

In 1923 architect T.J. Cullen won a contract for new civil offices from Kerry County Council. The building took four years to build at a cost of £32,480 and was opened to the public in March 1928. It was named after Thomas Ashe, who was born in Lispole, in west Kerry.

Today Tralee is a lively market town and shopping centre, particularly noted for Siamsa Tíre, the National Folk Theatre of Ireland, founded by Fr Pat Aherne. In 1991 Siamsa Tíre moved into a new theatre and arts centre with a design based on a 2,000-year-old Irish stone fort. The Rose of Tralee festival and the Tralee Races still attract capacity crowds. Two new attractions in the town are 'Kerry the Kingdom' which incorporates an audio visual presentation, the Kerry County Museum, the newly restored Tralee-Blennerville Steam Railway and 'Geraldine Tralee', an exhibition in the Ashe Memorial Hall which brings visitors back to the Tralee of 1450.

BRIEF BIBLIOGRAPHY

Annals of the Kingdom of Ireland by the Four Masters, trans. by John O'Donovan, 1860.
The Blasket Islands, Joan & Ray Stagles, O'Brien Press, 1980.
Killarney & South-West Ireland, Ward Lock's Red Guide.
Killarney & the South of Ireland, Mr & Mrs S.C. Hall, Miros Press, reprint 1976.
Discovering Kerry, T.J. Barrington Blackwater Press, 1976.
Listowel and its Vicinity, J. A. Gaughan, Mercier Press, 1973.
In the Kingdom of Kerry, Richard Hayward, Dundalgan Press, 1946.
Cork and Kerry, Sean Jennett, B.T. Batsford Ltd, London, 1977.
Austin Stack, J. Anthony Gaughan, Kingdom Books, 1977.
The Ancient and Present State of the County of Kerry, Charles Smith, 1756.
Blennerhassett Island in Romance and Tragedy, Minnie Kendell Lowther, Tuttle Publishing, 1936
The Sea Heritage of Dingle, Pádraig Long, 1988.
Tragedies of Kerry, D. Macardle, Irish Freedom Press, 1988
Killagha Abbey, Killagha Abbey Restoration Committee, 1991.
County Kerry, Past and Present, Jeremiah King, Hodges Figgis & Co, 1931
Selections from Old Kerry Records, Mary Agnes Hickson, Watson & Hazell, 1872.
A History of the Kingdom of Kerry, M.F. Cusack, 1871.
Dingle, Jack McKenna, Mac Publications, 1985.
Tarbert on the Shannon, D. & J. Holly, Donegal Democrat
Rambles Through West Kerry, Peter Locke, 1988.
Topographical Dictionary of Ireland, Samuel Lewis, 1837.
A Kerry Footballer, Mick O'Connell, Mercier Press, 1974.
Romantic Hidden Kerry, Thom F. O'Sullivan, Kerryman, 1931.
The Antiquities of the County of Kerry, John O'Donovan, Royal Carbery Books, reprint 1983.
The Reminiscences of an Irish Land Agent, S.M. Hussey, Duckworth & Co, London, 1904.
Napper Tandy, Rupert J. Coughlan, Anvil Books, 1976.
In Wicklow, West Kerry and Connemara, John M. Synge, O'Brien Press, 1980.
Valentia, Portrait of an Island, D. Pochin Mould, Blackwater, 1978
The Tralee and Dingle Railway, D. Bradford Barton, 1977.
A Guide to Blennerville, Frank Blennerhassett, Butler Sims, 1991
Causeway, Its Location and Legend, Jerry Allman, 1983.
Munster at War, Barry O'Brien, Mercier Press, 1971.
The Great Dan, C. Chenevix Trench, Jonathan Cape, 1984.
Kerry's Fighting Story. Anvil Books
A Visitor's Guide to the Dingle Peninsula, Steve McDonogh, Brandon, 1985.
Milltown, Denis Sugrue.
Castleisland, Rev. Kieran O'Shea.
A Dictionary of Irish History since 1800, D.J. Hickey and J. E. Doherty, Gill & Macmillan 1980
Knockaderry National Schools 1841-1988.
Ardfert Past & Present, Ardfert Youth Club, 1979.
Griffith's Valuation, county of Kerry.
The Origin and History of Irish Names of Places, P.W. Joyce, 1920
Journals, newspapers & directories
In and About Killorglin, Mid-Kerry.
The Kerryman.
Freeman's Journal.
Annascaul Fortlore, Fr John Ashe.
Antiquities near Lispole, Rev. R. Orpen.
The Kerry Magazine.
The Kerry Archaeological and Historical Society Journal.

GLOSSARY

Annals: *Chronicle of events.*
Black & Tans: *Formed in 1920 by British Government as an auxiliary force for Ireland. They wore khaki trousers and dark green tunics, and reminded people of Scarteen Black and Tan, a Limerick hunt.*
Bullaun: *A large boulder with hollows used for grinding grain.*
Caher: *A stone fort.*
Clochán: *(or beehive hut). A small stone building built of dry masonry in the shape of a beehive.*
Crannóg: *An artificial island in a lake or marsh used for defended dwellings.*
Cromlech: *A large capstone resting on three or more upright stones (also dolmen).*
Currach: *A small traditional craft used for fishing.*
Dún: *A fort.*
Fenians: *Irish revolutionary society established by James Stephens, 1858*
Gaeltacht: *District where the Irish language is still spoken.*
Fionn Mac Cumhaill and Fianna: *Legendary group of early Irish warriors led by the heroic Fionn.*
Gallaun: *A single pillarstone used to mark Bronze Age graves.*
Megalithic tomb: *Early Bronze Age tomb built from large stones.*
Milesians: *Early invaders to Ireland, believed to be from Spain.*
Ogham: *Alphabet of lines and dots cut on stone.*
Pattern: *A religious festival to commemorate a local saint, usually held on his feast day.*
Planter: *An English or Scottish settler given forfeited lands in Ireland by the British in the 17th century.*
Pillarstone: *Prehistoric single large upright stone.*
Rath: *Ring fort.*
Souterrain: *Underground passage close to a fort.*
Stone Circle: *A circle of stones indicating an ancient place of ritual.*
Tuatha Dé Danann: *Principal early mythical invaders, whose name means 'people of the Goddess Danu'*
Tír na nÓg: *land of eternal youth, mentioned in stories of the Fianna*
Ring fort: *A circular enclosure, bounded by ramparts and ditches*
Wedge tomb: *Rectangular-shaped chamber tomb.*
Station (religious): *Holy place, where prayers are said.*

PUBLIC REPRESENTATIVES FOR COUNTY KERRY

1st Dail, Dec 1918: *North* N.J. Crowley (SF), *West* Austin Stack (SF), *South* Finian Lynch (SF), *East* P. Beasley (SF).

2nd Dail, May 1921: The same candidates were re-elected.

3rd Dail, June 1922: The same candidates were re-elected.

(From 1923-35 Kerry was one constituency) Kerry/West Limerick.

4th Dail, Aug 1923: Austin Stack (AT), Finian Lynch (T), Thomas McEllistrim (AT), James Crowley (CnaG), Patrick Cahill (AT), T O'Donoghue (AT), John O'Sullivan (T).

5th Dail, June 1927: James Crowley (CnaG), John O'Sullivan (CnaG), Finian Lynch (CnaG), Thomas McEllistrim (FF), Austin Stack (SF), W. O'Leary (FF), T. O'Reilly (FF).

6th Dail, Sept 1927: James Crowley (CnaG), Thomas O'Reilly (FF), W. O'Leary (FF), F.H. Crowley (FF), Finian Lynch (CnaG), John O'Sullivan (CnaG), Thomas McEllistrim (FF).

7th Dail, Sept 1932: Eamonn Kissane (FF), Thomas O'Reilly (FF), F.H. Crowley (FF), Finian Lynch (FG), John Flynn (FF), Thomas McEllistrim (FF), John O'Sullivan (CnaG).

8th Dail, Jan 1933: Finian Lynch (CnaG), Thomas McEllistrim (FF), John O'Sullivan (CnaG), F.H. Crowley (FF), John Flynn (FF), Eamonn Kissane (FF), Denis Daly.

In 1935 County Kerry became two constituencies.

9th Dail, July 1935: *North* Stephen Fuller (FF), Tom McEllistrim (FF), John O'Sullivan (CnaG), Eamonn Kissane (FF). *South* Fred Crowley (FF), Finian Lynch (FG), John Flynn (FF).

10th Dail, June 1938: *North* Stephen Fuller (FF), Tom McEllistrim (FF), John O'Sullivan (FG), Eamonn Kissane (FF). *South* Fred Crowley (FF), John Flynn (FF), Finian Lynch (FG).

11th Dail, June 1943: *North* Dan Spring (L), P. Finucane (CnaT), Tom McEllistrim (FF), Eamonn Kissane (FF). *South* F.H. Crowley (FF), John Healy (FF), Finian Lynch (FG).

12th Dail, May 1944: *North* Dan Spring (L), P. Finucane (CnaT), Tom McEllistrim (FF), Eamonn Kissane (FF). *South* F.H. Crowley (FF), John Healy (FF), Donal O'Donohue (FF).

13th Dail, Feb 1948: *North* Dan Spring (L), P. Finucane (CnaT), Tom McEllistrim (FF), Eamonn Kissane (FF). *South* F.H. Crowley (FF), John Flynn (Ind), Patrick Palmer (FF).

14th Dail, May 1951: The same candidates were re-elected.

15th Dail, May 1954: *North* Dan Spring (L),

Tom McEllistrim (FF), P. Finucane (CnaT), Johnny Connor (CnaP). *South* F.H. Crowley (FF), John Flynn (FF), Patrick Palmer (FG).

16th Dail, March 1957: *North* Dan Spring (L), Tom McEllistrim (FF), P. Finucane (Ind), D.J. Mooney (FF). *South* Honor Crowley (FF), Patrick Palmer (FG), John J. Rice (SF).

17th Dail, Oct 1961: *North* Dan Spring (L), Tom McEllistrim (FF), P. Finucane (Ind). *South* Tim O'Connor (FF), Honor Crowley (FF), Patrick Connor (FG).

18th Dail, 1965: *North* Dan Spring (L), Tom McEllistrim (FF), P. Finucane (Ind). *South* Tim O'Connor (FF), Honor Crowley (FF), Patrick Connor (FG).

1966 By-election *Kerry South* John O'Leary (FF)

19th Dail, 1969: *North* Dan Spring (L), Tom McEllistrim (FF), Gerald Lynch (FG). *South* John O'Leary (FF), Michael Begley (FG), Tim O'Connor (FF).

20th Dail, 1973: The same candidates were re-elected.

21st Dail, 1977: *North* Dick Spring (L), Tom McEllistrim (FF), Catherine Ahern (FF). *South* Tim O'Connor (FF), John O'Leary (FF), Michael Begley (FG).

22nd Dail, June 1981: *North* Dick Spring (L), Denis Foley (FF), Tom McEllistrim (FF). *South* Michael Moynihan (L), John O'Leary (FF), Michael Begley (FG).

23rd Dail, Feb 1982: The same candidates were re-elected.

24th Dail, Nov 1982: The same candidates were re-elected.

25th Dail, Feb 1987: *North* Dick Spring (L), Jimmy Deenihan (FG), Denis Foley (FF). *South* John O'Leary (FF), John O'Donoghue (FF), Michael Begley (FG).

26th Dail, June 1989: *North* Dick Spring (L), Jimmy Deenihan (FG), Tom McEllistrim (FF). *South* John O'Leary (FF), John O'Donoghue (FF), Michael Moynihan (L).

27th Dail, 1992: *North* Dick Spring (L), Jimmy Deenihan (FG), Denis Foley (FF). *South* John O'Donoghue (FF), Breda Moynihan-Cronin (L), John O'Leary (FF).

FF	Fianna Fáil	FG	Fine Gael
L	Labour	CnaT	Clann na Talún
Ind	Independent	SF	Sinn Féin
T	Treaty	AT	Anti-Treaty
CnaG	Cumann na nGaedheal		
CnaP	Clann na Poblachta		

INDEX